Lisa

9/13/13

Peace

+

Love.

David Dyer

D*From*arkness *to*Light

DAVID L. DYER

BALBOA
PRESS
A DIVISION OF HAY HOUSE

ISBN: 978-1-4525-4882-1 (sc)
ISBN: 978-1-4525-4881-4 (e)
ISBN: 978-1-4525-4883-8 (hc)

Library of Congress Control Number: 2012904923

Balboa Press books may be ordered through booksellers or by contacting:

Balboa Press
A Division of Hay House
1663 Liberty Drive
Bloomington, IN 47403
www.balboapress.com
1-(877) 407-4847

Printed in the United States of America

Balboa Press rev. date:4/20/2012

Dedication

To my lovely wife, Janet
I don't think I would be sitting here writing this
book today without my beautiful wife, Janet.
She has been and is the rock behind me,
and she has endured so much.
I intend to work on repaying her each day
for what she has gone through.
Janet, I love you.

And to my loving son, David-Scott
You've shown me. Now show the world.

It is further dedicated to my brother,
Jim, and his lovely wife, Marilyn

And, of course, to my beautiful mother, Hazel
How lucky I am at the age of 73 to still be able to take my
mother to dinner and then watch a baseball game with her.

A special thank you to Karin Risko
for her editing assistance.

My Time to Touch
by David L. Dyer

When I vowed to give up alcohol,
Which was my lifelong crutch,
I was given a brand-new life.
It became my time to touch.

Dedication To Wayne

To my brother Wayne

Pull up a chair, sit down and relax
While I reminisce
There's not a single doubt in my mind
That you'll enjoy reading this

I'm going to go back in time a few years
To give this story some semblance
I really mean quite a few years
To my earliest remembrance

I remember the bed that came out of the wall
And reached almost to the door
And also how much fun we had
Playing marbles on the floor

Things that I have written before
I'll try not to repeat
Remember the days we would walk to school
To the end of Tucker Street

As you wrote in your book of Mr. Scarf's death
I, too, couldn't comprehend
His never returning home again
And what was considered the end

Add those thoughts to the story I wrote
About you at seven-years-old
How your actions stopped the bullying
A story I'm glad I told

There were many things I saw in you
At that very tender age
No matter how bleak things seemed to be
You could always turn the page

A few years later in Vietnam
I learned to comprehend
I saw death and destruction so many times
Yes, over and over again

Two years later on Okinawa
My thoughts of you were not clear
But for some unknown reason I felt
Your presence very near

The year was nineteen seventy-four
And we had drifted further away
Further than we we'd ever been
Until one summer day

You took a trip to Mississippi
To do what you thought was right
Soon you found yourself alone
At MLD's gravesite

You forgave him for what he had done
To us and to our mother
You had no knowledge of the effect
That this had on your brother

It was from that point, the drifting stopped
And began to turn around
And very soon I would find
Myself, homeward bound

Your words have inspired me
Through the years
Here are nine that helped me continue
As you looked me in the eye, you said
"Do not die with your music still in you."

Your brother, Dave

Foreword

The book you hold in your hand, written by my big brother David, is a masterpiece of just plain fierce honesty. And just like the dark secrets that could no longer remain obscured by my brother's silence, the truths revealed here, the stories you are about to read, had to be published in order for Dave to feel that he had finally, once and for all, emerged from the shadows that tormented his soul for over seven decades. My brother writes not because he seeks fame or fortune, and not to prove himself in any fashion. No. He writes because this is his way of slamming shut the door on a past plagued by self-imposed visions of fear, self-doubt, and pessimism. This is the guy I grew up with from the moment I was brought home from the hospital as a newborn.

My mother tells me about what that day was like. Our father had decided that he could not responsibly handle a family of three boys under the age of four, and thus, he had moved out and elected to move in with a girlfriend in a neighboring community. These were the early days—a depression, a war, an uncle being held by the Nazis in a POW camp in Europe, another uncle in a ship in the war-torn Pacific, and a mother stuck working as a candy girl at a five-and-ten-cent store, with a wayward, thieving, drinking man for a husband. A man who refused to work honorably and who ultimately opted to abandon these four struggling souls, refusing to look back and never even make a phone call.

David and I spent many years in foster homes, while our older brother, Jim, lived with our grandmother. Finally, we were all reunited in 1949 with a stepfather who also voted for alcohol, slovenly work habits, and eventually divorce, over being an accountable provider.

The first fifteen years of my life were spent with the man whose book you hold in your hands. We were inseparable. My portrait of my brother Dave is very much at odds with his own self-image. To me he was my everything—my constant companion, my big brother, my only friend. We were there to protect each other if needed. He slept right next to me in the same bed every night that I can remember. We played together, we talked about everything together, because the one thing that was a constant in our young lives, no matter where we lived or what the circumstances, was each other. He wasn't just my brother. He was an extension of me. It was always Dave and I.

Out of these experiences, in what I call the lean years, each of us took something that we needed for our life path. I was benefiting from these early paltry beginnings in preparation for becoming a teacher of self-reliance. Dave's life purpose was also at play. While I expressed myself outwardly, Dave turned inward. To me, he was the smartest guy in the world; to himself, he languished in self-repudiation. To me, he could do anything; to himself, he felt inadequate.

The series of stories you are about to read are all rooted in these early years. As we progressed through our teen years, my brother David became obsessed with his uncommunicativeness. To have a conversation with Dave after we were reunited as a family and for decades to come, well into his sixties, was a torturous path indeed. He would respond only with a short, one-word answer, and if I didn't continuously prod him, there would be stone silence. And yet this was a young boy and a young man who had many qualities that I considered to be genius. He created his own language; his droll sense of humor revealed a wit unsurpassed by anyone I have ever known. His heart was as big as the sky, and yet, upon close examination, it was severely broken as well.

Here in this collection of stories, Dave tells of his lifelong battle with alcoholism and addiction to cigarettes, and how he had chosen to drown his enormous potential for greatness in a sea of beer and clouds of hazy smoke from his three-pack-a-day habit.

His early memories are written out in a story format, largely I feel because he has kept them buried for so many years. He writes poignantly of these times when he felt such dismay over how he disappointed our mother, his brothers, and most tellingly, his own feelings of ineptitude and inadequacy. These feelings took him from the very edge of dependency, where his life was no longer worth living to him, and into a career in the Army.

As an enlisted man, Dave began to heal and then thrive, but he still took solace in his "best friend," his daily six- pack of beer. Some of Dave's most heart-rending writing involves his years in Vietnam, where he came face to face with the daily horrors of what it feels like to be a participant in such madness. He tells of holding the hands of young nineteen-year-old soldiers as they lay dying and the tears that it brought to him as he ministered helplessly to these unfortunate young boys caught in an evil web of killing that made victims of everyone involved in the insanity of war.

David buried these images somewhere deep within his psyche. I know because I was never able to get him to even talk about these horrific memories. And here he writes about them with the pen of a scholar and a poet. My brother, David, received the nation's fourth-highest medal for service in combat, the Bronze Star, something I only discovered some thirty or more years after the award ceremony.

David heard me say at a speaking engagement several years ago, whatever you do, "Do not die with your music still in you." It was shortly after this lecture that David was diagnosed with Parkinson's disease, attributable to his two years of service during the Vietnam War. Agent Orange was being spread indiscriminately throughout the entire country to destroy anything that might be alive, including unfortunately, many, many Vietnamese, as well as American soldiers.

I have often spoken about how the lowest points in our lives are often our greatest teachers. The storms of our lives often provide us with the equipment we need to climb to even more exalted heights. And so it was with my brother's Parkinson's disease diagnosis. Something happened to my brother Dave after the initial shock of this discovery. David finally decided that he indeed was not going to end this life's journey with his music buried within him. He began to discover the inner glow that had been concealed for the greater portion of his life. This brilliant man—who dropped out of high school, not realizing that he was entombing a sleeping intellectual giant and feeding him booze to keep him in that inner vault—was now going to be released.

David writes perceptively and with a new clear-headedness that had previously eluded him of all that he once refused to even mention. He writes poetically of his love for his family, for nature, and most stunningly of his having found God. Dave gives way too much credit to his "celebrity" brother for his remarkable awakening and his tender journey. This is a man whom I admire with all my heart. He is a war hero—not just because of what he did in service to his country, but because of his triumph over all of these battles that he writes about here in his emergence from darkness into the light. His triumph over early childhood illnesses; his victory over self-repudiation and depression; his amazing victory over that scary foe that takes so many people down, alcohol, something he battled for half a century and emerged a winner. His truly amazing victory over fear and his triumph of living in love with his beautiful wife and adoring son and his biggest conquest of all—his emergence as a spiritual messenger from his lifelong sojourn in the world of the sacrilegious.

This is my brother's story, and I am so proud to introduce it to you here in the Foreword to his own book. Did I ever tell you, Dave? You are my hero. I love you.

Your brother,

Wayne

Table of Contents

Preface   xix

Introduction   xxiii

Part 1 My Brother Wayne and Me

Chapter 1.   My First Memories   3

Chapter 2.   Mt. Clemens Musings   9

Chapter 3.   Summers in Sombra   15

Chapter 4.   Memories on Moross   21

Chapter 5.   Baseball and Bravado   27

Chapter 6.   Growing Up and Apart   33

Chapter 7.   The Furthest Point: Vietnam and Faces of Fear   37

Chapter 8.   My friend Lynda   47

Chapter 9.   Forgiveness and Its Rewards   59

Chapter 10.   A New Beginning   61

Chapter 11.   My Brother Helps Marry Me Off   75

Chapter 12.   The Power of Giving   79

Chapter 13.   Relinquishing the Music   85

Chapter 14.   Connection or Chance Encounter   89

Chapter 15.   Forgiveness Sets You Free   93

Chapter 16.   Nostalgic Ride Evokes Special Gift   97

Chapter 17.   Munificent Means Wayne   101

Chapter 18.   The Unbroken Bonds of Brotherhood   103

Part 2 My Time to Touch:Short Stories and Poems by David L. Dyer

Living with Parkinson's   109

A Revelation Or Something Happened This Past
    Christmas Eve   113

Play On Words   125

A Valentine to my Wife   129

Happy Birthday Connie   131

Nineteen Eighty-Six   133

To the Love of my Life   139

Spring   141

The Night before Christmas in South Vietnam, 1970   143

Preface

Oh my God! How many times have you used that expression? I know I use it every day. In fact, seventy-five percent of us probably react with "oh my God" whenever something either good or bad happens.

Today I experienced a profound oh-my-God moment when I sat down at the computer and attempted to retrieve my writings. Instead of finding all my hard work, I faced a blank computer screen.

Last night, my wife Janet reminded me it was Sunday night. For many households, Sunday night means gathering up the trash and taking it to the curb for early morning pickup. So last night I took care of the trash, which is my weekly chore.

I've been working on this book for three or four weeks, day and night. I do my writing in longhand and then enter it into the computer after a couple of pages. I seemed to be moving along fairly well, although at times I was somewhat apprehensive about whether I should or shouldn't be entering this or that. I'd often wonder, *What would Wayne think about it?* With Wayne in Hawaii and me in Michigan, I just couldn't be conferring with him at the turn of each page. I decided I should write this book in my own words.

I attempted to retrieve all that I had written on the computer up to that point so I could add the introduction I had just written, but all that appeared on the computer was a blank screen. I asked Janet for help, since she's much more knowledgeable about computers than I am. She couldn't retrieve my work either. Suddenly I thought about the trash and was overcome with dread. In the trash—which, incidentally, had already been picked up—lay my original longhand version of the entire book. Since I had already typed the entire manuscript and saved it to the computer, I'd thought nothing of tossing out my only hard copy of the book. I lost four weeks of time and effort: eighty pages and eighteen thousand words! They were gone and lost forever. Poof!

My hard work had disappeared—just as our father had disappeared when my brother and I were young kids. My mother had faced the option of giving up or starting over. It's obvious what choice she made, as we're alive and well this many years later. Now, at the age of seventy-two, I wasn't about to give up either—not when I had just begun writing three years ago.

Losing the initial material and subsequently rewriting this book must have been a message from my God, reminding me that I'm the author of this book and that it should be written by me.

Oh my God. That might sound like a strange way to begin a book. However, had I not realized and accepted the fact that there is a God, this book and any of the stories within it might never have been written. A very powerful force lies within me, one that I will call "my God" only because I know of no other word to use. It could very well be that everyone has this force within them.

You'll see how my acceptance of God has given me the strength to face a diagnosis of incurable Parkinson's disease at the age of sixty-eight and how that disease has become somewhat of a blessing. If not for this life-altering diagnosis, I would never have been able to tell the stories you are about to read—stories about my brother Wayne and me. They are true stories that only I can tell, because in our early years, we only had each other. Other than family members and close friends, no one has heard these before.

I'll show you how my little brother Wayne has influenced me throughout our lives, even though I'm eighteen months older. You'll see that even though we were inseparable during the early years, we grew far apart. Later our relationship underwent an abrupt turnaround that brought us back together, even closer than before.

—David L. Dyer

Introduction

"Do not die with your music still in you."

After hearing those words from my brother Wayne for about the fourth time, I was finally spurred into action. Let me begin by introducing Wayne. He's Dr. Wayne W. Dyer, the famous author of *Your Erroneous Zones* and many other bestselling books. A member of the International Speakers Hall of Fame, he's regarded by many as the "father of motivation." Throughout this book, you'll see how my younger brother Wayne's presence has inspired me throughout my entire life.

Yes, Wayne Dyer does have a brother. In fact, he has two of them. Jim is our older brother, and I—David Dyer—am the middle brother. We all share the same beautiful mother Hazel, who turned ninety-five years old in April 2011.

It was those nine magical and powerful words often uttered by Wayne—"Do not die with your music still in you"—that prompted me to release the music I have been holding within me for the past thirty-seven years. Those nine important words inspired me to relive the painful memories that Wayne and I shared as children, to confront the demons of my Vietnam years that have long haunted me, to acknowledge the fact that I'm an alcoholic, and to cope with my 2007 diagnosis of Parkinson's disease.

Those words encouraged me to face my past as well as a future dealing with a life-altering, incurable disease. They also inspired me to uncover a talent for words and writing that had lain dormant for years and to use that talent to tell my story. Those nine important words launched a new chapter in my life, where I experience great pleasure telling not only my own story but other people's stories as well.

I'll be telling Wayne's and my story throughout the pages of this book. Being the brother of a celebrity has always been very exciting, and I've always been so proud of him. Even at the tender age of seven, I saw and felt that Wayne possessed something special that would carry him well into the future. I certainly did not envision the magnitude of his success and popularity, but I did foresee a bright future for him.

We all have a story within us. Perhaps those nine magical words—"Do not die with your music still in you"—and our story will inspire you to tell yours.

Part 1 My Brother Wayne and Me

~

|| Chapter 1 ||

My First Memories

My story begins with my earliest memories. It was winter of 1942/43. We lived on Piper Street on the east side of Detroit. Wayne was two years old; I was four. My brother Jim, who was six at the time, wasn't there. He must have been at my grandmother's house.

There was a lot of snow and ice on the ground. Wayne and I were sliding around on the ice on the sidewalk in front of our home. When Wayne fell, my mother hollered at me from the upstairs window and told me to stop pushing him. A few minutes later, he fell again, and she yelled at me once more. The third time he fell, even though he had fallen on his own, we both had to go inside.

I remember playing marbles with Wayne on the floor of the living room. A Murphy bed was in the room. It seemed that whenever we pulled the bed out of the wall, it was so large that it filled up the entire room.

Why have I given so much ink to those two memories? For some reason, those are my earliest and only memories of that time period. This may seem strange, but my memory stops at that point, and I don't recall anything until age seven. I have no memory of ages five or six.

David L. Dyer

While I don't remember it, something tragic occurred when we lived on Piper Street. Our father walked out of our lives and left our mother to raise three young children alone.

My father never returned, and we never heard from him again. While I have no memory of him—I was only four when he left us—I've never heard anyone say anything positive about him. I do know that when he left, our family was broken apart. With a limited income, Mother had absolutely nowhere to turn for help except to her parents. My grandparents were able take one of us in. Jim went to live with them.

Over the next six years, Wayne and I would be boarded out to several different foster homes. We'd see our mother, grandparents, and Jim infrequently. Fortunately, Wayne and I weren't separated. We had each other and unto each other we clung.

Me, our mother Hazel, Wayne and Jim, Piper Street, 1942

*Jim, Wayne and me, 1942, around the
time our father abandoned us*

6

Wayne and me, Mt. Clemens

Me and Wayne, at the Sombra, Ontario cottage

‖ Chapter 2 ‖

Mt. Clemens Musings

Whenever someone mentions the city of Mt. Clemens, I immediately think of Wayne. I believe that Wayne, likewise, would immediately think of me. That's really amazing, considering that our time there was relatively short. In contrast, I spent almost twenty years of my adult life making the hundred-mile daily commute from my home southeast of Detroit to my job copying medical records at a Mt. Clemens hospital and back. Yet when I hear of Mt. Clemens, I don't think of the long drive or my former job. I think of Wayne, and the childhood memories come flooding back.

In September of 1946, Wayne and I were sent to live with Mr. and Mrs. Scarf and three or four other children at 231 Town Hall Road in Mt. Clemens, Michigan. Wayne and I were always together in those early days. We enjoyed doing kid-things, like listening to Joe Louis fights on the radio or cutting out pictures of baseball players and box scores from the newspaper and pasting them into scrapbooks. How I wish I had saved those scrapbooks!

Every Sunday, the Scarfs made us go to church. One of my fondest memories involves Wayne and me walking up Town Hall Road to the nearby Baptist church where we'd eagerly watch the newly saved get baptized. They were completely submerged in water, fully clothed and all.

Other vivid memories from Mt. Clemens include gathering eggs every morning and watching the chickens hatch. When the chickens grew into hens, they were fair game for dinner. Killing chickens became our job, so Wayne and I would scatter feed in the center of the coop. We'd grab a hen by the feet, take her to the chopping block, lop off her head, and watch as she flopped around for a couple minutes. Then we'd drop her into boiling water and pull off the feathers. Soon she became our Sunday dinner. This seemed to be an every-Sunday ritual. I can't imagine doing it today!

When Wayne and I arrived in Mt. Clemens, the first priority was enrolling us in school, which had already been in session for two weeks. Wayne, who was six, went into first grade. Since I would be eight in a month, I was placed in the third grade. Remember earlier when I mentioned that I had no recollection of ages five and six? To this day I have no memory of schooling prior to the third grade. I can recall, however, with great clarity the apprehension I felt when placed in a class of students who were older and had more schooling than me. The students were also physically much larger than me.

I didn't know it at the time, but I had been born with serious health issues. My mother had a difficult time carrying me during pregnancy, and I was born with a condition called anemia, a blood deficiency that may have resulted in my being unusually small for my age. It wasn't until my early teens that I would experience what's known as a growth spurt.

When my third-grade teacher introduced me to the class, I was no bigger than a first- grader. I can still hear the laughter today. Because of my size, I was ripe for bullying. It didn't take long for it to start.

Usually I waited for Wayne after school, and we walked home together. One day, I decided to walk home by myself. As I made my way home, I heard a bunch of kids behind me.

"Hey, there's a third-grader!" one of them shouted.

I started to walk faster.

"Let's get him!" they cried.

I started running. Before I knew it, I was on the ground. A first-grader was on top of me, swinging his arms and hitting me. I could do nothing but cry. When I finally freed myself, I ran home, locked myself in my bedroom, and cried for an hour.

I never told Wayne about that incident, which means I told no one. In those days, Wayne and I only had each other. We confided in each other about everything, but the bullying was just too humiliating—especially since I was a year and a half older than him and two grades ahead of him in school.

The bullying continued throughout the year, but it was never serious enough to do any physical harm. It did impact me emotionally and made me hate school. I spent more time dodging bullies than I did on schoolwork. That coupled with the fact that whatever was being taught always seemed to be over my head made for a truly miserable school experience.

The next year, when I turned nine and Wayne seven, he had pretty much caught up to me in size and strength. Wayne would never mention this or rub it in. In fact, he always looked at me as his "big" brother and would tell me and everyone else how strong I was. After we taught ourselves to play baseball, he always told everyone what a great ballplayer I was.

I never told Wayne about the bullying, and it never happened in his presence. I do think he heard about it, though, and suspected that something was wrong. One day after school, Wayne revealed to me that another kid was picking on him. Rather than keeping it to himself as I had done, Wayne told me. I admired his courage.

Wayne told this bully that he was going to get his big brother to beat him up. What was he thinking? I didn't know how to fight. How in the heck did he think I could beat anyone up? Besides, the boy was a third-grader and bigger than both Wayne and me.

Wayne calmly told me not to worry.

"You won't have to fight him; just scare him off."

What I'm about to write really happened. I believe this incident is a precursor to what Wayne's mission in life was destined to become. Remember, Wayne was only seven years old when he devised a plan for me to gain much-needed confidence by facing my fears and standing up to a bully. Wayne's plan at age seven already employed principles he talks about today, such as mind-over-matter and self-realization. Amazingly, his plan worked.

The next day Wayne and I approached the boy when he was alone. Although I was shaking in my boots and had no idea what I'd say or do, I walked up to him. The boy looked frightened as he stared back at me. I didn't have to do or say anything. It seems that Wayne's comments about my strength and age did the trick. The boy didn't stick around to find out if they were true. I'll never forget that bright, wide smile on Wayne's face when the boy ran off.

Word spread quickly about how tough Wayne's older brother was, and the bullying subsided for the rest of the time I was at that school, which was another full year. It was during this time that I realized there was something special in the future for Wayne. I could actually see or dream of Wayne walking into a room full of people, where his presence alone would light up that room.

I can't help but think that this early childhood incident also instilled in Wayne a sense of self-confidence and an early self-awareness of the power of projection, positive thinking, and self-actualization. He seemed to grasp these concepts naturally and practice them at a young age, although it would be years before he could fully understand or articulate them. Wayne had the uncanny knack, even back then, to see the strengths in me and others, even if we didn't see them, and then to make us believe in our abilities. This would become one of his strong traits that would lead him to where he is today.

Decades later, my wife Janet, my toddler son David-Scott, and I attended a local speaking engagement where Wayne was the featured speaker. We arrived early and mingled with the other guests. Excitement permeated the air as we all anticipated Wayne's arrival. Suddenly, it seemed as if the room appeared brighter. I turned slightly and there stood Wayne, smiling. For a moment I again saw that seven-year-old kid with his big, bright smile, who possessed a sense of self-awareness far beyond his years. I realized then that my vision or dream as a nine-year-old had come true too.

Not only did I stand up to a bully that year, but another exciting event occurred in fourth grade. Up to that point, I had hated school, and unfortunately, I was never able to move past this. That year, though, I experienced a brief moment of joy when I discovered that I possessed an aptitude for spelling.

One day the teacher told us to line up around the classroom. We were going to have a spelling bee. Every student was given a word to spell. If it was spelled incorrectly, they'd sit down. There I was, competing against classmates who had much more schooling than I did and who were up to a year older. Yet there wasn't a word given to anyone that I couldn't spell.

Yes, I won that contest and received a standing ovation. I beamed with pride and had never felt so happy. I went home and told Mrs. Scarf, but she didn't seem very interested. Of course, I told Wayne the good news. He was the only person with whom I could share what I call the greatest experience in my first ten years of life.

|| Chapter 3 ||

Summers in Sombra

While living in Mt. Clemens, Wayne and I didn't get to see Mother or Jim very often—certainly not often enough. One reason was that Mother didn't drive and had no way of getting to us. The separation of our family tore at her heart.

Mother worked at Chrysler, earning the typical female wage for whatever job she was doing. In those days, men made almost double the wages paid to females for the same job. My mother's greatest wish was to somehow reunite her family again. With this in mind, she finally decided to marry Bill Drury, a fellow she'd been dating for a couple of years.

There was, of course, a major stumbling block. Bill was Catholic. Since my mother had been previously married, they couldn't get married in a Catholic church. Mother told Bill that he'd have to give up his religion if he wanted to marry her. Finally he agreed, and they were married in my grandparent's Hurlbut Street home sometime in 1948.

Bill's mother Cora owned a cottage in Sombra, Ontario. I remember all of us going there in the summer of 1948. For Wayne and me, it was as if we were visiting some kind of Fantasy Island. We'd swim, fish, play baseball, listen to ballgames on the radio, and even learn to play pinochle.

Jim and Wayne seemed able to swim right away, but it didn't come easy for me. Although I enjoyed just being in the water, swimming wasn't one of my favorite sports or pastimes.

It did bother me that my little brother Wayne, who was a year and a half younger than me, could swim circles around me. He, of course, would never brag or say anything to make me feel bad.

A half a mile down the road from the cottage was the lake access where we swam. If we dove off the dock, the water was deep and over our heads. If we swam straight out about fifty feet, we'd reach the sand bar where the water was only waist high. Jim and Wayne would dive in, and within seconds, they'd be standing on the sand bar. There was no way I could swim fifty feet, so I'd dive in and get out right away. So much for swimming!

Other summer memories include watching the magnificent fireworks display on the Fourth of July, cutting the grass with a push mower, and playing baseball. Wayne and I played catch whenever we could. We'd even watch the local Sombra baseball team practice and run the bases for them. Jim met a girl named Ethyl that summer, so he was always preoccupied with her. Wayne and I were inseparable.

One afternoon, Wayne and I discovered a nearby gas station run by a guy named Bill. Whenever the Tigers games aired on the radio, we'd head over to the gas station and listen to the game.

We pretty much had free reign that summer. Mother, Bill, Cora, and Bill's cousin Margaret seemed to play pinochle at the cottage day and night.

When the first of September rolled in, we closed up the cottage for the year. Wayne and I returned to Mt. Clemens and the start of another school year. I was now in fifth grade and Wayne in third. As usual, I hated school and always seemed to be floundering. Perhaps if I'd been put in the first grade with Wayne when we'd first enrolled in school, things may have been different. I don't know why I kept getting passed to the next grade in spite of never doing anything in class and receiving failing marks in every subject except spelling.

One day Wayne came home from school, wanting to know what a "scurvy elephant" was. His teacher had called him that. Turns out that she had called him a "disturbing element," not a scurvy elephant.

When Christmas vacation came around that year, Wayne and I received wonderful news. We would not be returning to Mt. Clemens. Instead, Wayne and I were to go live with my Aunt Audrey and Uncle Stuart who lived on the same street as my grandmother. We'd finally be near our brother Jim. For the first time—and the only time, except for one year in high school—all three of us would attend the same school.

During Christmas vacation, Wayne and I took swimming lessons at the local YMCA. The four-day course culminated in a ceremony where all the students who swam the entire length of the pool were presented with certificates of achievement. This was a big event, and our cousins from Canada even came over to watch.

Wayne dove in and swam the entire length of the pool with no problem. It was my turn. I dove in but couldn't make it all the way to the other end of the pool. Halfway through, I had to get out of the pool and dive in again in order to finish the lap. I finally made it to the end, but I wasn't awarded a certificate. I was devastated.

That summer, on our first day at the cottage, I wanted to prove to Wayne that I could swim as well as he could. There was no doubt in my mind that I could now swim the fifty feet to the sand bar.

My plan entailed tearing off my clothes when we reached the dock, diving in, and swimming to the sand bar, all by the time Wayne would turn around. Well, I did exactly that, but by the time I swam at least fifty feet, I couldn't touch bottom. I swam further and still couldn't touch. I tried to keep swimming and remain afloat, but I felt myself being pulled under. I was exhausted and scared. I heard Wayne scream for help. No one seemed to be around. Suddenly, I felt someone grab my arm. Wayne had been able to alert a nearby boater who pulled me to safety. Had my rescuer arrived just a few seconds later, it may have been too late.

When Wayne and I returned to the cottage and told Mother what had happened, she wisely encouraged me to go back into the water as soon as possible in order to avoid being forever afraid of water. Later that afternoon, Wayne and I went swimming. When I got out of the water, I was covered with hives. The next day, I went into the water and again broke out in hives. From then on, every time I went swimming, I would experience an outbreak of the hives. It got to the point that even a sudden change of temperature could trigger an outbreak. Eventually, I just quit swimming.

In 1976, I was stationed at Fort Riley, Kansas, and lived in Junction City. Wayne was in town promoting his bestselling book, *Your Erroneous Zones*. He and his daughter Tracy were staying at the Travel Lodge down the street from me and invited me over for a swim in the pool.

Wayne told me to focus my thoughts on anything other than hives as we entered the pool. He kept talking to me, and I didn't have a chance to think about anything other than what he was saying. In fact, he was speaking so softly that I couldn't make out what he was saying, so I had to keep moving closer and closer to him.

Wayne purposely had drawn my attention to him. Before I knew it, I had been in the water for half an hour. When I got out of the pool and dried off, I couldn't find a single hive on my body. For the first time in twenty-seven years, I didn't experience a breakout of hives when I went swimming. Immediately I went back into the water for another half hour with the same results. Since then, I've enjoyed swimming and have never experienced an outbreak of hives again.

Swimming wasn't my favorite childhood activity, but baseball became a passion—something Wayne and I enjoyed immensely. The summer of '49 with its fantastic pennant race was one of the greatest seasons in the history of baseball. Author David Halberstam chronicled that special season in *The Summer of '49*, which I consider to be one of the best baseball books ever written. As kids, we didn't really follow baseball until the next year, but I recall two key games from that exciting season.

In April 1949, as Jim, Wayne, and I walked from Aunt Audrey's house to our grandma's, we passed by the neighborhood drugstore on the corner of Hurlbut and Vernor Streets, where speakers broadcasted the opening-day game of the Detroit Tigers. We could hear and feel the fervor of the crowd through the airwaves. The excitement drew us in, and we sat on the curb and listened to the entire game.

The Tigers had a rookie center fielder, Johnny Groth, who was branded a "can't miss" player. He kicked off the game with an inside-the-park home run, and later he hit another one.

Wayne and I caught the last game of the season while hanging out in Bill's gas station in Sombra. We dropped a nickel or dime—or whatever it cost—for a bottle of Orange Crush and spent the afternoon there listening to the game.

Boston Red Sox left fielder Ted Williams enjoyed another one of his terrific seasons. On the verge of winning his third Triple Crown, he was robbed of this opportunity that day when Detroit Tigers third-baseman George Kell got his third hit of the game. Both players ended the season with a 349 batting average, but Kell surpassed Williams' record by .003 of a percentage point.

Whatever the outcome of that season, one thing was for sure: Wayne and I were hooked on baseball.

|| Chapter 4 ||

Memories on Moross

It seems as if Wayne and I lived with Aunt Audrey and Uncle Stuart for more than eight months, but it was only that long. With Jim living with our grandparents just two blocks away, we got to see him all the time and didn't have to say good-bye for extended periods of time anymore as we had in the past.

I'd like to mention a couple of early memories I have of my brother Jim. Every day before school started at 7 am., the kids played a game called barney-door. The game involved one child running the entire length of the playing field without being touched by another. Wayne and I proudly watched Jim win that game. Not only did he become the barney-door champion, he became known as "the fastest kid in the school."

Another memory involves Jim's last day at Jackson Intermediate School where I also attended as a freshman. A dance contest was held in the gymnasium as part of the senior farewell activities. During the contest, if you received a tap on the shoulder, you had to sit down. Jim and his partner were the last couple dancing, and thus became that year's Dance King and Queen.

Many people might view those as trivial accomplishments, but somewhere in the background was a 12-year-old little boy with a big smile on his face. I had again watched my brother Jim take first place for a second time in two unrelated events at two different schools. I may have been the only person to have witnessed both events.

I fondly remember Jim teaching me to ride a two-wheel bicycle at nearby Water Works Park. I'll never forget the sense of pride I experienced when I showed off my bike-riding skills to Mother. Other memories I recall include Wayne, my cousins Tom and Linda, and I walking to the Deluxe Theater to watch the latest movie releases, or sitting on the couch with Aunt Audrey, watching TV late into the night until the "Star Spangled Banner" played.

In August of 1949, we moved to a house on Moross Road and were finally all together again as a family. The downside was having our stepfather Bill Drury as a member of the family. Bill was an alcoholic and not a pleasant person to live with. We all pretty much walked around on eggshells in his presence.

Jim, Wayne, and I shared a nine-by-nine bedroom. Jim and I shared a bed, while Wayne slept alone in this tiny bed that was barely big enough to hold him.

Wayne and I attended Arthur Elementary School, which was within walking distance. I was in sixth grade and Wayne, the fourth grade. Jim attended Jackson Intermediate School for seventh and eighth grades. I would join him there the following year.

All three of us were expected to go to Sunday school every week. I, of course, hated the thought of going to any kind of school, whether it was Sunday school or regular school. I would do anything to avoid going to either.

Jim and Wayne probably figured if I didn't go to Sunday school, why should they? So Sunday mornings found us rising early, shining our shoes, and putting on our Sunday best—before heading out the door with no intention of going to church.

Usually we'd hang out at the drugstore on Harper Road and use our collection money to buy ice cream and comic books. We'd pass the time leafing through magazines, including the "girlie magazines" located much higher on the racks, out of the reach of children. I'd clasp my fingers together and bend forward. Wayne would step into my clasped hands, and I'd lift him up so he could reach those magazines. If memory serves me correctly, I believe we gazed at the first *Playboy* magazine, which featured Marilyn Monroe as the Playmate of the Month.

Jim, who was two years older than me and three and a half years older than Wayne, had his own circle of friends. Wayne and I made friends with several neighborhood kids and played baseball on Lanark Street every day from dawn to dusk. We lived for baseball and had so much fun that summer.

In the fall of 1950, I entered the seventh grade at Jackson Intermediate School. Jim was in the second half of eighth grade. He'd leave for Denby High School in January. Wayne attended fifth grade at a new school, Marquette Elementary, that opened in our neighborhood.

Jackson was four or five miles away, so I had to take the bus. I really wanted to go to Marquette Elementary, because Wayne and most of my friends went there. Being a new school, they didn't have a seventh-grade class. To be honest, I wouldn't have minded going back to the fifth grade. At least I would have been with kids my own size, and I might have even learned something.

Thus began what I call my double life or "dual persona," as my personality at home and school became polar opposites.

Jim and I had different schedules, so I walked to catch the bus at Morang and Worden every day alone. Without friends or my brothers, I kept to myself and again fell victim to bullying. It wasn't too bad, but just the fact that the bullying was allowed to exist made it bad enough. I hated to go outside for recess. At one point, I actually paid the biggest kid thirty cents a week for protection.

That winter, within a two-week period, two humiliating experiences further solidified my hatred for school.

One frigid day, I made the twenty-minute walk to the bus stop, only to find myself stuck waiting another half an hour for the bus to come. When the bus finally came, I was so cold that I began to break out in hives. By the time I arrived at school, I was covered with red bumps. Now, can you imagine how eleven- and twelve-year-old kids would react? They laughed, called me names, said I had cooties, and pretended not to come near me for fear of catching something.

The second time I broke out in hives occurred one morning when I arrived late for school and saw the classroom door shut. I couldn't bear to walk in late and bring any attention to myself under ordinary conditions, let alone with my face covered with red blotches. I just knew they'd laugh at me. Instead, I left school and endured what seemed like the longest day of my life. Outside in the cold, I walked around for six hours until the bus came to pick me up.

Bus rides were no refuge from bullying. The same group of guys owned the back of the bus. Every day, they'd block the bus driver's view and have fun by picking on somebody new.

School became unbearable, but I kept everything to myself. I began skipping school at least once a week to avoid the torment. I'd catch a ballgame or see a first-run movie at a theater downtown. The failing grades on my report cards reflected my despair. More than once, I changed the grades before getting my mother's signature. I'd change the grades back before returning the cards to school. Despite my bad grades, I was still promoted to the eighth grade.

In contrast to school, home life was a joy. The disparity between those two worlds seemed like night and day. At home, I had my brother Wayne and our neighborhood friends. These kids didn't laugh at me; they laughed *with* me.

I used my knack for words and began making up fun nicknames for all the kids. I strung together words and created sentences that had no meaning. We called it the secret language from the Land of Forgen. None of the kids could ever repeat the sentences without laughing. To see all the kids enjoying themselves, mainly because of my humorous antics, was so different from the ridicule I faced at Jackson.

‖ Chapter 5 ‖

Baseball and Bravado

Baseball ruled the summer of 1952. Wayne always played third base, and I played first. At times he fired the ball to me with such force that if I didn't catch it in the webbing of my glove, I'd almost get knocked down. That was one sore spot I endured, both literally and figuratively, whenever I played catch with him. Remember, I was the older brother and felt I should be the one to throw the ball harder.

It was when Wayne and I lived in Mt. Clemens that we discovered a love for that game and taught each other how to play it. I can remember spending hours cutting out box scores from the newspapers and pasting them in scrapbooks. When we moved to Moross at the end of the baseball season, we readied ourselves for the following season by placing baseballs in the pockets of our gloves and tying them tightly in place.

In 1952, spring seemed to come early. Now, when I use the expression "playing on Moross," that means playing on the island that separated the east and west sides of the road. The island was large enough to play catch and even football, a game we also enjoyed.

On a spring-like February day of that year, Wayne and I played catch on Moross. Soon a couple of other kids joined us. One of those kids was huge for his age and towered over the rest of us twelve- and thirteen-year-olds.

We joined this new friend at a local gymnasium where we learned to play basketball. This kid already knew the game and seemed better at it than anyone else. Believe me, I'm not making this up! He told us about an American Legion Baseball League where he was playing in the thirteen-to-fourteen-year-old division. We decided to join the league too and rounded up enough kids to create a team. It just so happened that we played our first game against this same kid, who was still only twelve-years-old. No one could hit his pitches. He seemed to strike out just about everyone he faced.

When I look back on this even today, I'm so proud to say I was able to stand up to the plate and take my three swings from this guy. Yes, it was an honor to have known, befriended, and played baseball and basketball with Dave DeBusschere.

Dave became an All State baseball and basketball player at Austin High School. He was also an All-American at the University of Detroit and went on to enjoy a Hall of Fame career with the New York Knickerbockers. Dave eventually became the Commissioner of the American Basketball Association. It was truly an honor to have known one of the greatest athletes of our time.

Dave, however, wasn't the only neighborhood kid to make his mark in sports. Let's jump forward to the 2006 World Series playoffs, where the Detroit Tigers faced the St. Louis Cardinals. In a game that requires about 75 percent luck and 25 percent skill and knowledge to compete for the big prize, I not only competed in the 2006 World Series fantasy league, but I won first place over several thousand teams. In addition to winning the $5,000 first-place prize, I was placed in their Hall of Fame.

Imagine three young boys, ages twelve to fourteen, who had played catch on Moross Road in the early fifties, all winding up in Halls of Fame in three completely different categories: Dave DeBusschere for basketball, Wayne Dyer for international speaking, and David Dyer—well, why not?—for fantasy sports!

While baseball and sports were bright spots in my life, school was still something I dreaded. Wayne sensed that I had problems and was bound and determined to find out what was wrong. Finally, I admitted to him how much I hated school and revealed that my hatred stemmed from always being one of the youngest and smallest kids in the class and a constant target for bullies.

Wayne responded by showing me an ad in a Superman comic book that intrigued me. The ad showed a ninety-seven-pound weakling at the beach getting sand kicked in his face. When that weakling finally decided he had taken enough abuse, he turned himself into Charles Atlas and exacted his revenge.

After that, Wayne and I started working out together and launched into an intense fitness regimen that included running, weights, push-ups, and sit-ups. All the exercise, along with playing baseball and football, seemed to quickly get me into pretty good physical shape.

It was at this time in my life that I learned of the anemic condition I'd been born with and how it may have stunted my growth. By coincidence—or what I like to call "connection"—I experienced a major growth spurt. The exercise and growth spurt created quite a noticeable change in me when I returned to school in the fall. As a self-confident eighth-grader, I wore short-sleeved shirts whenever I could and would squeeze my arms to show off my muscles. There was no more bullying for me.

Recess was no longer a source of dread for me, especially when it was announced that we would play softball at recess. With my experience from "my other life," there was no doubt that I was one of the best—if not the best—softball player at school. Unfortunately, even with my newfound self-confidence, the negativity I equated with school remained. I still disliked school and would continue to skip class at every opportunity.

On the last day of school, I learned that I had failed the eighth grade due to poor marks in economics and history. If I wanted to attend Denby High School in the fall, I'd have to enroll in summer school and repeat those classes.

This news really ticked me off. How would I tell Mother and Bill? On the way home, I sat by myself on the bus, contemplating this predicament. The bullies, seated in their favorite spot—the back of bus—were oblivious to my problems and need for quiet. In fact, it seemed like they were louder and more obnoxious than ever. Annoyed, I yelled for them to "shut up."

Then I got up and started to walk back there with the intention of just talking to them.

I was really in no mood to deal with these morons, but as I approached them, I remembered the lesson I had learned from my brother Wayne a couple of years earlier. The only way to put an end to the harassment was to face the bullies head on.

I'm not exactly sure how things transpired, but I think this account is pretty accurate. The ruckus prompted our bus driver to turn around and yell at us. When he yelled, the bus swerved and caused me to stumble into one of boys. As I tried to regain my balance, I grabbed tightly onto his shirt. The bus lurched, and I inadvertently pulled both of us back hard and accidentally smacked his head on the other side of the aisle. My elbow hit another guy squarely in the mouth and knocked out a tooth.

It looked like I'd beat these guys up all by myself, but the credit actually goes to the bus driver. If he hadn't swerved and knocked me around, I'd have been dead meat. There was complete silence after that as I made my way back to my seat. I was scared to death. I thought for sure I'd have to pay for that tooth. As it turned out, to the best of my knowledge, I never saw any of those boys again.

I attended summer school and moved on to ninth grade at Denby High. High school didn't change my negative perception of school in any way. I had no interest in it whatsoever. In September of 1955, I entered my senior year at age sixteen. One month later, I turned seventeen and never went back to school again.

During our teen years, Wayne and I began to drift apart. For the first fifteen years of our lives we had been inseparable. Now, with new friends and different interests, our relationship changed dramatically.

‖ Chapter 6 ‖

Growing Up and Apart

While I attended Denby High, I worked part-time in the produce department at Chatham Supermarket, a local grocery chain. When I quit school, I received a ten-cents-an-hour raise for becoming a full-time employee—sixty cents an hour, forty hours a week! I thought I was a big shot. When I turned eighteen, Mother got me a job at Chrysler through people she knew. This was a very good-paying job and an excellent opportunity, especially for an eighteen-year-old dropout. I, however, was too immature to realize this. I preferred to party, and I went out drinking every night until the early morning hours.

Wayne, on the other hand, had goals and a bright future unencumbered by the lure of alcohol. Wayne graduated from high school and joined the Navy, just like our older brother Jim.

My penchant for partying took a toll on my mother. There'd be nights when I'd come home at three a.m. and sleep in the car if I didn't have my house key on me. On more than one occasion, Mother found me sleeping in the car and begged me to come inside. She even wrote Wayne several letters, telling him about what she had to endure with me. So distraught was my mother that Wayne offered to seek an emergency leave from his post in Guam if she needed him.

Not only did my drinking and late nights negatively impact my family, but my work performance suffered, and I acquired a terrible driving record. It's a good thing drugs weren't as prevalent then as they are today, or I might not be here.

The following incident relives some rather painful memories where I know I hurt and disappointed the two people I worship, my mother and Wayne, and solidified the separate courses Wayne and I would travel.

The year 1960 was probably the worst year of my life. I quit my job at Chrysler, and with no particular goals, I floundered and whiled away the time drinking. On this particular Friday or Saturday night, I stopped in the Candlelight Bar in Harper Woods. I met up with four or five friends, and we drove around looking for girls and places to hang out. Throughout the night, we stopped at several different parties. I was twenty-one so there was no problem getting booze. Between the four or five of us, we bought several bottles of hard liquor, such as whiskey, Scotch, or bourbon. As the night progressed, we'd each take a swig from the bottle and pass it around until it was empty.

I must have consumed two bottles myself. I became so sick that I threw up everything inside me and then passed out completely. I had no idea how I even got home. I found out later that my friends had dragged me from the car and dumped me on the steps of my house. Can you imagine what my mother must have felt when she answered the knock at the door, found me lying there, and saw a car racing off?

The noise awakened Wayne, who was home on furlough from the Navy, and he came downstairs. Together, they pulled me inside the house. The next thing I remember, I was standing in the shower, fully clothed, with the water running full-blast over me. I must have sobered up a bit and began making stupid comments. The next thing I remember was Wayne's fist hitting me so hard that it knocked me out again. I know that punch probably hurt Wayne as much as it hurt me.

The next day I woke to the worst headache and hangover ever.

The following day, when completely sober, I volunteered for the draft and entered the service. The Army was the change I so desperately needed at that time in my life. I had thought about enlisting for quite some time, but it took that humiliating incident for me to realize that my life was going nowhere, and I needed to act. For once, I made the right decision. Being drafted turned into a rather illustrious twenty-one-year military career.

The night before reporting for my Army induction physical, I looked for someone to have a few beers with. I went to the Candlelight Bar and a couple of other hangouts but couldn't find anyone.

The Tigers' game was on the radio, and this was the legendary Ernie Harwell's first year broadcasting the games. It was during the second inning when I spotted the Cadieux Café and went inside to watch the game on TV. I watched this game with great interest, even though the Yankees had already clinched the pennant. Even though I had no one to share my pleasure with, it was a great feeling to see Roger Maris hit his sixty-first home run of the year and Norm Cash clinch the batting championship with a .361 average.

In reality, I wasn't alone that night. I was, in fact, accompanied by what would eventually become my very best friend, which would further be known as my six-pack.

It was at that time that Wayne's and my relationship became further strained and distant. When Wayne enlisted in the Navy, I only saw him a few times in the period before I joined the Army. Like the incident mentioned above, those times weren't always so great. The first ten of my fourteen years in the Army were spent overseas. We talked on the phone or saw each other perhaps two or three times during those years. Although we couldn't have been further apart, the bond couldn't be broken.

‖ Chapter 7 ‖

The Furthest Point: Vietnam and Faces of Fear

The years and distance would test and tug at the ties that bound Wayne and me. Eventually our relationship would again come full circle and become stronger than ever. Even during our periods of furthest separation, certain incidents kept us connected. Although Wayne would not be nearby during the most horrific and disturbing period of my life, his words later would again give me the strength to face the agonizing memories that would haunt me for decades.

The day after my twenty-third birthday, I was drafted into the US Army and committed to two years of service. After a year, I decided I wanted to travel the world, so I reenlisted for three years and went to Germany, where I was introduced to medical records, which would become my specialty and, later, my career as a civilian. When those three years ended, I reenlisted for six more years. At that point, there was no doubt that I would remain in the Army for twenty or more years.

In April of 1970, I received orders for Vietnam. There's no question that my years in Vietnam would become the most significant and disturbing part of my Army career. The harrowing situations I witnessed would take years before I was able to talk about them.

It took thirty-seven years after leaving Vietnam to tell my story. The incurrence of Parkinson's disease at the age of sixty-eight, some private counseling, and nine magical words from Wayne began releasing all that I had suppressed. Those words? *Do not die with your music still in you.*

My son David-Scott recently gave me a birthday present. Yes, it is something to wear. A half smile accompanied the tears that rolled down my face as I stared at the numbers engraved on the beautiful bracelet my wife Janet placed on my wrist. Those numbers read 58267, and they represent the total number of Americans killed in Vietnam.

In August 2007, at the age of sixty-eight, I was diagnosed with Parkinson's disease. When Wayne heard the news, he was devastated. He also sensed there was something I'd been holding back that was much deeper than this life-altering diagnosis. He sent me a motivational tape he had made with his publisher, Louise Hay. On this tape were nine simple words that were formed into a sentence. Without a doubt, it was those words, "Do not die with your music still inside you," that would entirely change my life.

I had always avoided talking about Vietnam, simply because there was nothing pleasant about the experience worth talking about. That reasoning may have been my way of avoiding any conversations that had to do with my experiences, since I just couldn't bring myself to talk about them without welling up. Instead, I would just revert to my comfort zone, which was my daily six-pack.

After hearing those words from Wayne and realizing that I now had this incurable disease, I began thinking about my mother, who was nearly ninety-two and lived in an assisted-living home in Florida. With me being ill and living in Michigan, the chances of us ever seeing each other were becoming very remote. I listened to Wayne's tape once again, and when those nine words again came to the fore, I immediately began taking action.

That very evening, I told Janet and David-Scott my Vietnam story and revealed the nightmares that have haunted me for the past thirty-seven years. I then wrote down this story and shared it with Wayne. He suggested I begin talking about my story whenever I can. Here is my story as I lived it and remember it.

On April 3, 1970, as the wheels of the plane touched the tarmac, I was never so scared in my life. We had just arrived at the Tan Son Nhut Airport in Saigon. Yes, I was in Vietnam. Yes, there was a war going on, and there was no escape. I had been in the Army eight years now. My specialty was medical records, and all my previous assignments had been at medical facilities.

About ninety percent of the men on this plane were lower-ranked and well-trained infantry men. They numbered in excess of 250. Most of them had more combat training than I did, even though they only had about a year of service behind them. Because of the staff sergeant stripes on my arms, they looked up to me. For that reason, I attempted to conceal my face of fear.

The bewildered and fearful faces on many of these young men were justified. The percentages dictated that ten of them would not make it back. Twice that number would be med-evacuated, and twice *that* number would suffer minor wounds.

I was assigned to the 71st Evacuation Hospital in Pleiku, which was located in the Central Highlands of Vietnam along the Cambodian border. Soon I'd discover the horrors of working in an evacuation hospital located within a combat zone where some of the heaviest fighting of the war took place.

I think I failed to hide my fear when the captain announced: "Welcome to Saigon, and I wish the best of luck to all of you in the coming year. The temperature is 89 degrees."

It took almost six days to get to Pleiku. On my first day there, I encountered my first DOA (dead on arrival), a young man dead from a self-inflicted gunshot known as a T&T (through one side of the head and out through the other side). Upon the sight of this DOA, I grabbed hold of the gurney where he lay to gain my composure. I stared at his face. He was only twenty-three. What had this war done to him? I took his clothing to our baggage room to inventory and secure his personal effects. As I looked through his wallet, I viewed photographs of what appeared to be his family members, as well as a pretty, young girl who may have been his wife or girlfriend. My eyes welled with tears, and a lump constricted my throat.

That night I returned to the barracks and locked myself in my room, where I cried my eyes out. I even prayed to God. I remember saying: "God, if you are a God, please help me get through this coming year." I didn't know it at the time, but God was there with me.

I soon learned that there was no time for mourning. My time to cry would come many years later. I vividly remember the MASCALs (mass casualties). One helicopter after another brought in sheer numbers of young men with mutilated bodies. They screamed with pain. Dozens of gurneys packed the ER (emergency room). The floor was covered with blood. Body parts were strewn about. Dead bodies were lined up outside, awaiting transport to the morgue.

I cringed as I listened to the moans and screams of the wounded. My heart wrenched to hear them begging for morphine to ease their pain. Those cries mixed with the orders shouted by understaffed and undersupplied physicians and nurses who had no room to move in this crowded emergency room. The screams and shouts would haunt me for years to come.

One of the most difficult decisions physicians had to make was to determine the priority of which patients should go into the operating room (OR) first. Because of the volume, many seriously wounded patients had to wait. Many died while waiting. I vividly recall one young patient who had received severe abdominal wounds and whose leg was separated at the knee. This nineteen-year-old did not survive the long wait for surgery and died in the emergency room. Witnessing this tore at my heart, but like everything else, we had to keep moving on.

All patients had to be admitted, and that was when my staff and I went to work. As casualties were brought into the ER, we put wristbands on them with a preassigned number for identification purposes. We would then interview patients for pertinent information and collect and secure their personal effects.

Three letters, MFW, which stood for *multiple fragment wounds*, was the most common initial diagnosis patients received upon admission. Many of the MFWs were in or near the abdominal area, a result of one of the favorite Viet Cong weapons used known as a Bouncing Betty. I have no idea where that name originated, but it refers to a land mine that shoots up an explosive charge to waist level before detonating. The intent was to strike at the private parts, which it often did.

When the time came to view the DOAs and secure any personal effects prior to taking them to the morgue, I began to see the real faces of fear. The image of ultimate fear is one that few people ever encounter. When a person is killed instantly, their body freezes in place and there is no movement. What that means is that their final thought is captured and frozen until it is changed by human hands. When a person sees death coming, that split second of overwhelming and paralyzing terror becomes etched on his face, and the ultimate face of fear is created.

41

In March 1971, the war began to wind down, and it was time to turn the hospital over to the Army of South Vietnam (ARVN). At this time, I voluntarily extended my tour for six months. I think my primary motivation for doing this at the time was a thirty-day non-chargeable leave. I was headed home for thirty glorious days. Prior to boarding the plane in Saigon, we were briefed about what we might encounter when arriving at the airport back home. This would be war protestors and the like. We were told to ignore them.

Most of the troops on this flight had completed their year of service and were going home. When we landed at the SEA/TAC terminal in Washington and deplaned, many of them actually got down on their hands and knees and kissed the ground. They were so happy to be home.

We did encounter what looked to me like a bunch of freaks. They were yelling obscenities and calling us killers in an attempt to get our attention. Even the security patrol told us these people had a right to protest as long as they didn't cross a certain line. It sounded like security was on the protestors' side too. It was not a very pleasant welcome-home for those of us who had just spent a horrendous year in Vietnam. Unfortunately, this was not an isolated incident. I wondered if those fools had any idea that Americans were dying over there every day for their freedom. I would equate their behavior to that of bullies in schools, and they were always in a group. While we Americans have the right to protest or speak out against a war, those actions should be limited to Washington, DC, where those decisions are made—not at the homecomings of those who have chosen or have been chosen to serve.

When I returned to Pleiku, I found that our hospital had become an inpatient medical detachment with a capacity to care for thirty patients. Our staff had been cut to the bare minimum, with most of our initial personnel either reassigned or sent home. My department included myself and one other person. As Murphy's Law would have it, within a couple of days, our small staff faced a horrific MASCAL. At first, I didn't think we'd be able to make it through. However, seeing the plight that overburdened nurses and physicians faced, we did all we could—especially since this came upon the heels of one of the most horrifying experiences I would ever encounter.

The morning prior to the MASCAL, we had received a body bag. The stench from that bag was so intense, we could smell it as it was unloaded from the helicopter, a distance of around two hundred feet away. We donned gas masks and proceeded to open the bag. Inside we found the bodies of three Americans stuffed inside a single bag. As we removed the body parts, the pilot, who had recovered the bodies, described how their heads had been placed on top of the bag. I can't even describe what was stuffed inside their mouths. To me, the impact of this incredible desecration of human life went far beyond any horrors I had previously witnessed, including the ultimate faces of fear. I could only imagine how much these brave soldiers had suffered.

When the siren went off that night, we again began receiving patients. Chopper after chopper dropped them off. That night I broke the pact I had sworn to uphold when I'd first arrived in Vietnam. For my own sanity and survival, I had vowed not to get personal with any of the patients.

A patient who had sustained burns over ninety percent of his body had been placed with the DOAs. I could hear him moan as if he were calling out to me. Doctors assured me that this young man was in no pain, and nothing short of a burn center could help. Even that would only prolong his agony. I knelt down and touched him. In a very weak voice, he asked me if he was going to die.

A few seconds later, with one final breath, he uttered one word: "Mom." In that very instant, I thought of my own mother and broke down. I couldn't see the fear in his face. All that was visible to me were the whites of his eyes. No, I didn't see the fear, but I felt it.

In August 2008, David-Scott and I visited the Vietnam Memorial in Washington, DC. This was absolutely the most moving experience of my life. I would suggest that anyone drafted during the Vietnam era visit this memorial and recite this modified adage in prayer: "Here, but for the grace of God, went I."

While I was there, I stared at the wall. All I could see were names and numbers. I closed my eyes, and then I began to see faces. I began seeing young men on gurneys lined up in the emergency room. Young men in body bags. Young men in psychiatric wards. I saw the young man with a self-inflicted gunshot wound that tore through his head. I finally saw the twenty-two-year-old burn patient who had died in my hands while crying for his mother with his last breath.

Yes, the nightmares have ceased somewhat since I began writing and talking about my Vietnam experiences. I do continue to have momentary lapses at times. Recently Janet and I attended a Michigan State University football game. Just prior to kickoff, the MSU marching band played one of the most beautiful versions of our national anthem that I have ever heard. Prior to the last stanza, they paused for a few seconds. While my eyes fixated on those Stars and Stripes, my thoughts took me back to Vietnam. That "moment" found me cringing as I approached a baby-faced man of twenty-two whom I swear didn't appear to be a day past seventeen. Now what could possibly be pleasant about placing death tags on his right toe and left thumb?

Many people have said and continue to say that the Vietnam War was not a popular war, and we shouldn't have been involved in it in the first place, since it was a war we couldn't win. Of course, it wasn't a popular war. Has there ever been a popular war? The word *popular* means "to be liked by most people." What war has ever been liked by most people? As far as the "should-haves" and "could-haves," just drop them completely and look at the reality. We soldiers were there! It was not *our* mistake for being there.

There are two more words that should be clarified in that previous paragraph. The words "we" and "our" refer to all those that donned the uniforms of the Army, Air Force, Navy, Coast Guard, and especially the Marines who stepped foot on the soil of Vietnam. If mistakes were made, they were political and were made in Washington, DC.

On this coming Memorial Day, Veteran's Day, and every day, let's remember those 58,267 Americans who gave their lives. Remember also that 39,996 of them were twenty-two years old or younger. Just look at the futures that were destroyed. We may even have lost a future president. Incidentally, there is a Vietnam veteran who did not die, nor did he become president. He did, however, come very close to dying, and he came very close to becoming president.

When I left Vietnam, my next assignment was at the US Army Hospital on Okinawa. I worked in the medical records section of the registrar division. Shortly after I arrived, I was given a special project. After being given a confidential alphabetical listing of the names of all the POWs that would soon be set free and return through Clark Air Force Base in the Philippines, I was to initiate their medical records. When the project was completed, somewhere in the middle of that stack of records was a record on a person named John McCain. It could have been John Smith for all we knew at that time.

Once again, back to those 58,267. Every one of them had a mother, father, other family members, and friends. Could you face any of those mothers and tell her that we shouldn't have been in Vietnam and that there was no reason for her son's death? Of course not! Look at the reality. A typical soldier was only twenty-two. He was drafted. He was sent to Vietnam. He was killed in the war. He died with honor. Forget the politics of right or wrong. Give him that benefit.

When soldiers' remains were returned home, those faces of fear were no longer visible. They had been changed by human hands to a look of solemnity. Again, as I gaze at my bracelet, I continue to see that ultimate face of fear. Those men died with honor. Honor them with your heart.

During my three years on Okinawa, I witnessed three historic events. I saw the dollar sink from 360 yen to under 200 when the island was officially returned to the Japanese. A twenty-five-cent taxi ride into town now cost two dollars.

The next big event was the release of American prisoners of war. I was in charge of initiating the POW medical records.

In 1973, Kentucky Fried Chicken opened up a franchise on Okinawa. One Sunday afternoon, I looked up from my desk at the hospital information center. Lo and behold, who stood before me? The real Colonel Sanders, clad in his white suit and carrying a cane, was standing there. I had no idea there even *was* a real Colonel Sanders, so for me it was like seeing Santa Claus. As a retired army colonel who had started his successful business long after he retired, the Colonel was there to visit another retired sergeant who was a patient at the hospital.

When my stint on Okinawa ended, I was sent back to the states. After many years apart, my brother Wayne and I would finally be reunited briefly, and I would discover that the special skills I'd always known he possessed had evolved into the start of something big.

‖ Chapter 8 ‖

My friend Lynda

I met Lynda Vandevanter in April 1970. Although I never saw her again after that month, she had a profound influence on me, one that continues even today. After signing into the 71st Evacuation Hospital in Pleiku, I was given a tour of the hospital and introduced to some of the people I would be working with. After touring the emergency room, we stopped by the break room used by the operating room staff. It was there that I was introduced to Lynda, an attractive, 23-year-old nurse.

Lynda had been in Vietnam for nine months and had three more to go before she could go home. She was being transferred to the 67th Evacuation Hospital in Qui Nhon, which was located about 60 miles south of Pleiku. We talked for a few minutes that day and then again the next day as we relaxed by the swimming pool. I may have seen her three or four more times in the hospital before she departed for the 67th Evac in May. Then, I never saw her again.

It wouldn't be until I retired from the Army in 1982 that I would hear Lynda's name mentioned again. It turned out she had written a memoir, a compilation of letters she had written mainly to her parents and family while stationed in Vietnam. Her book, *Home Before Morning,* was the inspiration behind the TV series, "China Beach" which ran for 64 episodes. In 1988, HBO aired the special *Dear America, Letters Home from Vietnam* which featured two letters from Lynda's book.

Below are the two memorable letters from Lynda's memoir *Home Before Morning* included in the HBO program.

"24 July 1969

Dear Family

Things are going fairly well here. Monsoon is very heavy right now---haven't seen the sun in a couple of weeks. This makes the sky much prettier at night when flares go off. There's a continual mist in the air which makes the flares hazy. At times they look like falling stars, then sometimes they seem to shine like crosses.

At 4:16 A.M. our time the other day, two of our fellow Americans landed on the moon. At that precise moment, Pleiku Air Force Base, in the sheer joy and wonder of it, sent up a whole sky full of flares—white, red and green. It was as if they were daring the surrounding North Vietnamese Army to try and tackle such a great nation. As we watched it from the emergency room door, we couldn't speak at all. The pride in our country filled us to the point that many had tears in their eyes.

It hurts so much sometimes to see the paper full of demonstrators, especially people burning the flag. Fight fire with fire, we ask here. Display the flag Mom and Dad, please, every day. Tell your friends to do the same. It means so much to us to know we're supported, to know that not everyone feels we're making a mistake being here.

Every day we see more and more of why we're here. When a whole Montagnard village comes in after being bombed and terrorized by Charlie, you know. These are helpless people dying every day. The worst of it is the children. Little baby-sans being brutally maimed and killed. They never hurt anyone. Papa-san comes in with his three babies—one dead and two covered with fragment wounds. You try to tell him the boy is dead—"fini"—but he keeps talking to the baby as if that will make him live again. It's enough to break your heart, and through it all, you feel something's missing. There! You put your finger on it. There's not a sound from them. The children don't cry from pain; the parents don't cry from sorrow; they're stoic.

You have to grin sometimes at the primitiveness of these Montagnards. Here in the emergency room, doctors and nurses hustle about fixing up a little girl. There stands her shy little (and I mean little—like four feet tall) Papa-san, face looking down at the floor, in his loin cloth, smoking his long marijuana pipe. He has probably never seen an electric light before, and the ride here in that great noisy bird (helicopter) was too much for him to comprehend. They're such characters. One comes to the hospital and the whole family camps out in the hall or on the ramp and watches over the patient. No, nobody can tell me we don't belong here.

Love,

Lynda"

Now go back to the second paragraph of her letter where she states that two fellow Americans landed on the moon at 4:16 A.M. Vietnam time. She further stated that she watched from the emergency room door. At that precise moment, I was watching those two fellow Americans land on the moon while sitting at a table at the NCO club at Fort Belvoir, Virginia. I had no idea at the time that exactly nine months later I would

David L. Dyer

be standing at that same emergency room door in Pleiku, Republic of Vietnam, right next to Lynda Vandevanter while patients were being received and triaged.

If this first letter didn't get to you, this next one certainly will. To really comprehend what it was like at that particular hospital, the story should be told by an operating room nurse. This next letter was Lynda's story of how she spent Christmas during her unforgettable year of 1969.

"29 December 1969

Hi, All

I don't know where to start except to say I'm tired. It seems that's all I ever say anymore. Thank you both for your tapes and all the little goodies in the Christmas packages. Christmas came and went, marked only by tragedy. I've been working nights for a couple of weeks and have been spending a great deal of time in post-op. They've been unbelievably busy. I got wrapped up in several patients, one of whom I scrubbed on when we repaired an artery in his leg. It eventually clotted, and we did another procedure on him to clear out the artery—all this to save his leg. Well, in my free time I had been working in post-op and took care of him.

When I came in for duty Christmas Eve I was handed an OR slip—above knee amputation. He had developed gas gangrene. The sad thing was that the artery was pumping away beautifully. Merry Christmas, kid, we have to cut off your leg to save your life. We also had three other GI's die that night. Kids, every one. The war disgusts me. I hate it! I'm beginning to feel like it's all a mistake.

Christmas morning I got off duty and opened all my packages alone. I missed you all so much, I cried myself to sleep. I'm starting to cry again. It's ridiculous. I seem to be crying all the time lately. I hate this place. This is now the seventh month of death, destruction and misery. I'm tired of going to sleep listening to outgoing and incoming rockets, mortars and artillery. I'm sick of facing, every day, a new bunch of children ripped to pieces. They're just kids—eighteen, nineteen years old! It stinks! Whole lives ahead of them—cut off. I'm sick to death of it. I've got to get out of here.

Peace

Lynda"

Even today I occasionally open her book and read a page or two. It makes no difference which of the 382 pages I open it to, it keeps the memories of the 71st Evacuation Hospital and the 58,267 men and women who gave their lives during that war alive. I now wear a bracelet on my wrist with that number engraved as an everlasting memory.

After her book was published, Lynda went on to launch and become head what was called the Vietnam Veterans of America Women's Project.

Since Lynda's letters recall the traumatic experiences of Vietnam, there is a subject I want to address – the psychological syndrome called post traumatic stress disorder, otherwise known as PTSD. Simply put, PTSD is a delayed reaction to severe stress.

It's common for victims of catastrophic experiences to immediately suppress their feelings after experiencing horrific events. While this may enable these victims to cope in the immediate aftermath, these feelings do not remain suppressed. They come back in a variety of physical, emotional and interpersonal ways.

Studies have shown that Vietnam Veterans who were victims of PTSD had severe problems which included depression, rage, anxiety, sleep disturbances, recurring nightmares, instability, flashbacks and more. My question is how could we not suppress our feelings? We couldn't stop and mourn for every dead body we came across. This would be especially true with Lynda.

51

If that is the profile of PTSD, then I certainly am a victim myself. I found solace from those memories in my daily six-pack. Now, since my Parkinson's diagnosis, I've been able to replace the six-pack with my writing which has helped me to articulate those long pent up feelings.

In Lynda's case, she was one of the first female veterans to be diagnosed with PTSD. She also suffered from a vascular disease which was attributed to wartime exposure to chemical agents and pesticides. It was 32 years after the day we met, that my friend Lynda died at the very young age of fifty-five.

Thank you Lynda for sharing your memoirs.

*Wayne's 1958 high school
graduation photo*

Wayne, Jim and I at Jim's wedding

Me, 1961 basic training photo

Me, 1970, stationed in Pleiku, Republic of Vietnam

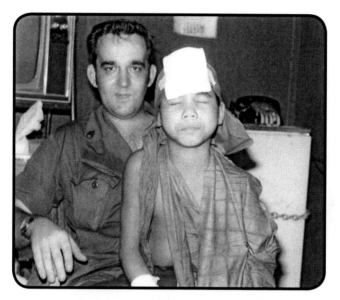

*Me and our adopted Montagnard boy
whose entire family was killed*

My Bronze Star Award

*Me, 2008, proudly wearing my Vietnam
Veteran's hat after visiting "The Wall"*

Another photo of me at the Vietnam Veteran's Memorial Wall in Washington, DC

‖ Chapter 9 ‖

Forgiveness and Its Rewards

In the summer of 1974, Wayne would experience a personal revelation that would enable him to claim his past and move forward to create his own future. At that time, Wayne was thirty-four years old, and I was thirty-five—the exact midpoint of our lives and the furthest point apart we'd ever drifted in our relationship.

After the Navy, Wayne had attended Wayne State University, where he laid the groundwork for his distinguished career as a counselor and therapist. After earning his doctorate, Wayne worked as a professor of counseling education at St. John's University in New York. He published articles in educational journals on positive thinking and motivational techniques, and he started his own private therapy practice.

Perhaps it was his own teachings—that we can take control of our own lives—that prompted Wayne to examine his own past and to confront the father who had abandoned him when he was only two.

Jim, Wayne, and I all have our own opinions and images of Melvin Lyle Dyer, our biological father (whom I refer to as MLD), and they're probably all different. Why wouldn't they be? None of us knew him. He walked completely out of our lives when we were just little kids. He walked out, never to return or to be heard of again.

Throughout our lives, Wayne has had many thoughts of MLD, much more than I ever did. He seems to struggle with those thoughts even today. That year, Wayne did some research and discovered that MLD had died from cirrhosis of the liver in 1964 and was buried in Biloxi, Mississippi.

In June 1974, Wayne found his way, as he has so often written and talked about, to MLD's grave. As he walked toward the grave, he was filled with hatred for this man who had walked out on our family so many years ago. Then Wayne had a revelation. "This is my father, and no one has ever had anything good to say about him." Immediately, Wayne's hate turned into love. He forgave MLD for all he had done or hadn't done—to himself or for our family.

That healing experience seemed to propel Wayne onto an exciting new path in life. Shortly afterward, he wrote and published his first book. It became the bestselling book of the decade, and he went on to a decades-long career that still inspires people throughout the world, even today.

I also believe that, at the same time, Wayne forgave me—his older brother who was stationed halfway around the world—for drinking, partying, and causing so much grief for my mother. My brother Wayne had grown up admiring me, and I had turned into a man he didn't really like or recognize. But from the point when Wayne forgave MLD and me, our once-distant relationship began to heal, and we moved toward restoring the closeness we had once shared when we'd only had each other.

‖ Chapter 10 ‖

A New Beginning

In 1974 I returned from my final assignment in Okinawa. Before reporting to Fort Riley, Kansas, I returned to Michigan and my mother's Sterling Heights home to spend my three-week leave.

Upon my arrival, Mother told me that Wayne would be speaking at a nearby church the following week. She further explained that people would be coming from miles away to hear him talk.

What could he possibly be speaking about in front of all those people? I thought to myself. I had been in the Army for twelve years and out of the country for most of those years. I had never heard Wayne speak.

On that day, Mother and I arrived for Wayne's sold-out speaking engagement. The church was packed with many guests who were forced to stand. When Wayne walked onto the stage, he received an enthusiastic ovation like I had never heard before.

I was awestruck. This was the little boy who had slept with me for so many years, the same little boy who had traced the letters of words on my back—as I had done on his—while listening to Joe Louis fights on the radio. He was the same little boy who had spied with me on Pat, the daughter of one of our foster parents, as she strolled naked down the hallway before taking a bath.

As Wayne talked about overcoming guilt, fear, worry, etc., I turned around and watched the audience in amazement. He held that audience in the palm of his hands. During the two and a half hours he spoke—without notes or a break— the audience fixated on his every word. Without personal prejudice, I can say that it was the greatest lecture I have ever heard. Someone else must have been listening too, because Wayne would eventually be elected to the International Speakers Hall of Fame and become known as the Father of Motivation.

Later that night, Wayne and I had a chance to catch up. He mentioned that he was writing a book and asked if I had any ideas for the cover. I didn't have any suggestions but told him I'd think about it.

A few months later, while stationed at Fort Riley, excerpts from his book began appearing in the National Enquirer. Every time a new magazine came out, I'd run up to the bookstore and buy up all the copies to pass out to everyone at the hospital. His book, a little thing called *Your Erroneous Zones* published in 1976, became the bestselling book of that entire decade.

Suddenly, the relationship between Wayne and me began to return as strong as ever. In 1976, Wayne crisscrossed the nation to promote his new book. On the way to a television appearance in Kansas City, he stopped by Junction City to visit me and spend the weekend. It was during this visit at the Travelodge that Wayne helped me overcome the outbreak of hives that long plagued me whenever I went swimming.

I attended the taping of his television appearance in Kansas City that included the governor of Missouri. I remember that the governor, who came on the show after Wayne, said, "He's a hard act to follow."

From that day on, I followed Wayne's career and never missed an opportunity to see or hear him speak.

In December of 1982, I retired from the military and moved back home to Michigan, residing in an apartment near our mother. Soon afterward, with lots of help from Wayne, I purchased a small condominium. He was still looking out for me, and this would be one of many generous gifts my brother Wayne would bestow on me over the years to come.

Janet and I on our wedding day, 1986

The Toga Party - 1985

Me, Wayne's daughter Serena and Wayne

Janet, Wayne, Me with David-Scott, 1995

*Wayne, me, Janet at one of Wayne's
seminars at the Church of Today*

Wayne and I with our mother Hazel on her 75th birthday

Me, Mother, Wayne and Jim

Me, Wayne, and Jim

Wayne, his daughter Tracy and me,
1976 , Junction City, Kansas

Janet and me enjoying life

*David Scott and me after he completed
the 2010 Chicago Marathon*

Janet and me aboard a 2011 Hay House cruise

me

Wayne

‖ Chapter 11 ‖

My Brother Helps Marry Me Off

Though not deliberate, my brother Wayne even had a hand in how I met my lovely wife Janet.

It was March of 1985, and I was living alone in the condominium Wayne had helped me purchase. Tired of being alone, I felt it was time for a change in my life. Just as Wayne taught, I decided that in order to bring about a positive change in my life, I'd have to take action.

This was a big step for me. The shyness that had afflicted my youth had followed me well into my adult years. Plus, my drinking habit had turned me into a very private, unsocial person. Although the ugly incident where I'd been dropped drunk and unconscious on my mother's porch steps had prompted me to enlist in the Army, it hadn't made me quit drinking. Throughout the years, especially during my Vietnam days, I had found solace in alcohol—so much solace that I jealously guarded my private time so that I could be alone with my dearly coveted, daily six-pack.

Even so, I knew I was missing out on something special in my life. I wanted to meet someone who could fill that void. Back in the eighties, singles ads in magazines and newspapers were prevalent, as were singles' outings and clubs. I took a leap of faith and responded to a couple of ads in one of the papers. A few days later, a gal named Clara responded. Her letter intrigued me enough to call her and set up a date to meet over coffee.

Well, we met for coffee, and the first thing Clara asked was if I was related to Dr. Wayne Dyer. When I explained that he was my brother, she perked up and became very interested. It was evident there were no initial sparks between either of us, but I could sense she wanted to know more about Wayne. I, of course, was happy to oblige as I always was proud to show him off.

Clara told me how Wayne's book, *Your Erroneous Zones*, had helped her through some recent problems. While I wasn't attracted to Clara, I loved to talk about Wayne and was proud of his success. I told Clara that Wayne would be in town the following week to speak at the Church of Today. I invited her to attend with me and mentioned that we'd get front row seats and possibly the opportunity to have lunch with Wayne. Clara accepted the invitation. As promised, we sat up front and dined afterward with Wayne at a nearby restaurant. Clara seemed to have enjoyed the entire day including the opportunity to meet and dine with Wayne. So how did Clara's letter lead to me meeting my wife? As I drove Clara home, she invited me to an upcoming toga party—another popular thing from the eighties—that her singles club was throwing. I'd never been to toga party before, so I said yes.

The next day, however, I noticed that Georgetown had made it to the finals in the NCAA Basketball Tournament, and the game would be televised on Saturday night, the same day as the toga party. I had followed Georgetown closely, ever since I'd been stationed at the Pentagon in 1981. While stationed there, I had even attended a high school All-American game in which Patrick Ewing played. In this upcoming tournament, he would be playing against the great Michael Jordan and North Carolina for the NCAA title. I couldn't miss that game. It wasn't like today, where you can press a button and watch the game later. So I called Clara and begged out of attending the party.

Over the next couple of days, I thought more about the toga party and what I might be missing. Intrigued, I decided, the heck with the basketball game. I called Clara to tell her I'd attend.

The day of the party, I met with Clara, and she helped me create a toga out of a sheet. Once we'd arrived at the party, I discovered that Clara was one of the party organizers. She quickly left me to fend for myself as she greeted guests as they arrived. I felt completely lost standing there, not knowing anyone except Clara.

The music started and people began dancing. I wasn't much of a socializer, especially around a bunch of strangers, but I had my buddy—a beer in hand—so I was all right. I noticed a young lady nearby who seemed to be alone amongst a bunch of strangers just like me. I invited her to dance.

Her name was Janet. As I began to introduce myself, she interrupted me. She already knew who I was. Janet knew that Wayne was my brother and that I had taken Clara to see him speak. She even knew that Clara had dined with us.

It turned out that Clara had invited both of us to the party. Janet was actually a friend of Clara's and was staying at her place for the weekend. Had Clara set us up to meet?

Janet and I seemed to hit it off right away. Although Janet appeared to enjoy my company, she seemed guarded and concerned about Clara's feelings. Did Clara like me and want to date me? Janet did give me her phone number, and when I called the next day, she agreed to a date. The rest is history. Janet and I have been married twenty-six years and have a wonderful son, David-Scott.

Was fate at play? I don't know. I do know that Clara probably wouldn't have been interested in me if my brother hadn't been Dr. Wayne Dyer. If I hadn't offered to take Clara to Wayne's speaking engagement, she probably wouldn't have extended an invitation to the toga party that resulted in my meeting the love of my life. So unbeknownst to Wayne, he inadvertently played another major role in my life and helped me meet Janet.

‖ Chapter 12 ‖

The Power of Giving

In August 2007, I was delivered a huge blow. I was diagnosed with Parkinson's disease, an incurable degenerative disorder of the nervous system. My first symptom occurred that month in the midst of my weekly exercise regimen. During my daily four-mile walk on the treadmill at the YMCA, something I did five times a week, my arms weakened and my right leg totally collapsed beneath me, forcing me to lose balance and control of my body.

I had never before experienced such a loss of control. I managed to stay in a prone position by grabbing hold of the sidebars on the treadmill and willing myself to stay upright. I stayed in that position for about ten minutes, trying to rest and regain control.

I honestly thought I was having some kind of stroke, although I didn't have any chest pains. I managed to hide this episode from everyone else at the gym, even though I was sweating profusely. They probably assumed my perspiration was from exertion; otherwise someone surely would have called an ambulance.

A few minutes later, I eased myself off of the treadmill and slowly attempted to take that first step, fearing I might not have any movement in my legs.

Very carefully I made my way home. When I got there, I lay down on the couch and slept for about two hours, until the phone rang and woke me up. I jumped up to answer it and realized I was walking just fine, as though nothing had happened.

Two days later I had to drive to Flint for business. One-hundred-mile trips one way were not unusual for me. My job as a medical records specialist in the private sector entailed lengthy commutes to hospitals throughout Michigan. These drives were no problem at all for me.

I drove to Flint, conducted my business and drove back. I was almost home when I remembered that I needed to stop at the library and return a book. I walked to the front door of the library, where I lost complete control of both legs and collapsed on the ground.

Luckily, a kind lady walking behind me helped me up. I didn't break any bones or draw blood, but I was shocked and shaken. This was the second time in two days I had experienced a complete loss of control over my body. I had no idea what was wrong with me. Again, after a few minutes I seemed to be fine, and I drove the rest of the way home.

I had an appointment with my cardiologist in two days, so Janet and I decided I would stay home and rest until the appointment. It then dawned on us that we were supposed to meet our son David-Scott at the annual Renaissance Festival in Holly, which would be another two-hundred-mile round-trip drive. Two broken legs would not have kept me from seeing our pride and joy, so we decided to make the trip as planned.

I felt fine and drove the hundred miles there. Janet would drive us back. We made it there without incident. When I tried getting out of the car, however, I knew something was seriously wrong. I couldn't stretch my legs out to walk even one step at a time. Every attempt to move was met with excruciating pain.

Janet drove me to the gate, where we met up briefly with David-Scott before heading back home. I kept my Tuesday doctor's appointment, and my cardiologist ordered an emergency consult with a neurologist. Dr. Garg conducted a nerve test, gave me some medication, and advised me to return in seven days. When I returned a week later, I was given the devastating news. I had Parkinson's disease.

From my experience with medical records, I knew what Parkinson's disease was and what would happen. I knew what I had to do to control it, but I wasn't ready. I didn't take the news well, though I put on a good front for others. Of course, I told Janet, my mother, and anyone who asked that the medicine was helping. In truth, it was having the opposite effect.

I wouldn't let the medicine help. Depressed, disillusioned, and angered by this life sentence of an incurable disease, I looked again to alcohol for solace. All I cared about was my next beer. I'd start drinking at two p.m. every day, and by seven p.m. I would be on my eighth beer. I'd eat something then and be in bed by eight p.m. every night.

The medication combined with my drinking brought back vivid Vietnam memories as if I were reliving them in the present—memories that I had continuously concealed for thirty-seven years. I'd see myself receiving the Bronze Star, the nation's fourth-highest award for service in a combat area. Then I'd see images of a burned soldier and wonder, *What did he get?*

What *did* he get—that young burned-to-a-crisp, twenty-two-year-old who had died in my hands while crying out with his last breath for his mother? I, a perfect stranger, had been the only one to hear that desperate plea. That young man must have had a very loving relationship with his mother to think of her with his final breath. And I'm the one chosen to keep his memory alive, but I don't even know his name.

I'd see the images of the thousands of others who had their names posthumously engraved on a wall in Washington, DC. I might add that it took eleven years for this to even happen. Again, I'd see myself receiving the Bronze Star; but those who had made the ultimate sacrifice by giving their lives—what did they get?

By late September, I had sunk into the deep abyss of despair. I became so sick to my stomach that I had to drink a beer to relieve the pain. One day I actually got down on my hands and knees and prayed to God, just as I had been taught to do when I was four-years old. It was probably the first time I had done it since then. The most I think I got out of that prayer was the desire to believe. Suddenly, I felt I had to find out what it meant to believe and begin living it. After that revelation, it didn't take long for things to change for the better.

On the morning of October 1st, my phone rang. At first I wasn't going to answer it, because I was about to leave for a business trip to Adrian, a drive I now dreaded but had to make. If I timed it right and left at exactly ten a.m., I'd be back by two p.m. and could start drinking. Honestly, that was how bad my drinking was. Finally, worried I might miss an important call; I answered the phone on the fifth ring. Thank goodness I did. Not only was that call important, it was the start of a positive transformation.

My brother Jim was on the phone, calling with a proposition I couldn't refuse. To surprise my mother for Christmas, he wanted to bring me and my family down to Florida to visit her. He would put us up in a hotel and cover all our expenses, including the gas to travel there.

I was elated. Janet and I were both only working part-time. With the expenses of a big home, we had lots of bills. A vacation was at the bottom of our list. After hanging up with Jim, I drove to Adrian and back and actually enjoyed the drive. I called Janet on the way, and she was thrilled.

In retrospect, I'm so glad Jim called when he did. If he'd waited to call until after eight p.m., he would have caught me around the time of my nightly drunken stupor, and I probably wouldn't have talked to him.

Another amazing thing occurred during that drive. When I told Janet about the trip, we decided to rent a vehicle so we wouldn't put excess miles on our car.

Halfway home, Wayne called me on my cell phone to let me know he had purchased tickets for Janet and me to attend his fiftieth high school reunion with him the following October. He might also be in town that weekend for a speaking engagement.

Wayne had absolutely no knowledge of Jim's call or plans. When I told him, he was just as excited as I was. Think about this for a minute. Our mother was ninety-two-years-old at the time, and I had just been diagnosed with Parkinson's disease. The odds were not in favor of my Mother and me ever seeing each other again. Jim must have put an awful lot of thought into that "gesture of love," which would eventually be the title of a book I would write and give to Mother. The thought of writing that book for my mother also lifted my spirits tremendously.

As I told Wayne about our plans to rent a car for the Florida trip to save wear-and-tear on our car, he said without hesitation to trade in our van for a new one. Just like Jim's gift to help me see Mother, it didn't take long for me to accept Wayne's offer.

Janet, David-Scott, and I drove to Florida in our new Chrysler Pacifica. We enjoyed spending our first Christmas in years with Mother, Jim, and Jim's wife Marilyn. The trip wasn't a cure-all, but it was the start of a new attitude. Jim's call had given me a reason to smile and be happy, something I hadn't done or been since my Parkinson's diagnosis several weeks earlier. It's amazing how powerful the gift one gives can really be.

‖ Chapter 13 ‖

Relinquishing the Music

After my Parkinson's diagnosis, I tried to avoid any meetings with Karen Lobbs, the lovely lady with whom I had worked for over twenty years. Several times she invited my family to her home in Traverse City, but I didn't want her to see me in my current physical state. I just continued to do my job, although my hours had been drastically reduced because the company had recently downsized.

On a few occasions, I mentioned doctors' appointments as excuses. The following February she called and asked me to be honest with her about my medical condition. I revealed that I had Parkinson's disease. Being in medical records like me, she understood the severity of this disease. She then revealed to me her recent lupus diagnosis.

Like kindred spirits, we talked at length about our medical problems, feeling free to confide in someone who understood what we were going through. As if the symptoms of our life-altering illnesses or the side effects of the medicine weren't enough to cope with, the mid-winter blues seemed to exacerbate our frustrations.

The very next day, out of the blue, Wayne called. I told him about the conversation I'd had with Karen. He told me about a tape he had just recently made with Louise Hay, another internationally acclaimed inspirational author and speaker and the founder of Hay House Publishing.

He would send me two copies of his new book and corresponding tapes. One autographed set was for Karen. Karen's birthday was the day after Valentine's Day, and David-Scott was to be in a play that weekend at Alma College, mid-state. We invited Karen and her husband Jerry to join us for the play and to stay overnight in the local hotel. We had adjoining rooms and celebrated her birthday with a small party after midnight. We met again for breakfast at the local Big Boy restaurant. It really made me feel good to be able to treat Karen and her husband that weekend. The whole outing seemed to lift her spirits. Just seeing her smile lifted mine.

Upon returning home, I finally had the opportunity to listen to Wayne's tape for the first time. Wayne talked about Martha, one of the girls from our youth who had left me with a lifetime remembrance of her—that being a one-inch scar on my wrist where she accidentally stabbed me with a paring knife. He talked about our life in Mt. Clemens, and for the umpteenth time I heard him repeat those words: "Do not die with your music still in you." Suddenly it seemed as if those words were directed to me alone.

At that moment, those nine words hit me so hard that I actually dropped to floor and sobbed uncontrollably. That same evening, I sat Janet and David-Scott down and revealed to them the music I had held within me all these years. I talked about the pain of being separated from my family and boarded off to strangers, the intense bullying, and of course, the memories that haunted me most my Vietnam years. A couple of days later, I repeated the story to Wayne, and he urged me to write it down or put it on tape and repeat it as often as I could.

After unleashing the story within me, the urge to visit the Vietnam Memorial or "The Wall" in Washington, DC, became overwhelming. David-Scott and I decided to make the trip. With my Parkinson's disease, it took nearly an hour for David-Scott and me to make the mile walk from our hotel to the monument. It was worth every step.

We must have stayed at the Wall for several hours. There David-Scott and I engaged in a lengthy heart-to-heart talk, and he presented me with a Vietnam veteran's cap, a gift I'll always cherish. I vowed to return to this site again and proudly wear the hat he so thoughtfully gave me.

Without question, this visit would become one of the most moving experiences of my life. It was there that I truly appreciated the gift of life I had received. I vowed then and there, on the steps of the Vietnam Memorial, to give up alcohol and embrace my remaining years of life in memory of those 58,267 who were never given that opportunity. By the way, the average age of those 58,267 killed in Vietnam was twenty-three.

|| Chapter 14 ||

Connection or Chance Encounter

When David-Scott and I returned home from our trip to the Vietnam Memorial, I began writing my story, or what Wayne calls "music," in earnest. I began with a tribute to my mother called *A Gesture of Love*, a collection of short stories covering the years of my life when I was drafted into the Army back in 1961. My mother and I had a loving but rather distant relationship. I hoped the book could bring us closer.

My original thoughts were to give her the book for Christmas. Somehow, though, I felt an internal pressure to complete it earlier. Wayne would be in town in October for his class reunion and speaking engagement. I wanted to have the book finished by then.

That October, Janet and I met up with Wayne at a local hotel to attend his class reunion and motivational seminar. I brought Mother's book with me. The night of the reunion, we waited for Wayne in his hotel room along with his secretary Mia. Wayne was delayed, and we still needed to get ready for the party, so we left. I left Mother's book in the room. Mia must have given it to Wayne.

At the party, Wayne told me he had glanced through the book and would return it in the morning. I personally don't think he glanced through it; I believe he read the whole thing. The next day as he began his seminar, Wayne introduced me to the audience. He had been devastated when he'd heard of my recent diagnosis of Parkinson's disease, and it's my perception that he was subconsciously hoping that someone would step forward and offer assistance.

Like always, when Wayne finished the seminar, he autographed his books and spoke with fans. As Janet and I headed for the lobby, I heard an unfamiliar voice calling my name. I turned around and saw a very nice-looking woman walking toward me. Her name was Connie Fedel. Connie teaches yoga to senior citizens with special needs.

Ironically, Connie had left her house that morning without a business card. She had returned home to retrieve a card, because she had a feeling she was going to meet someone at the seminar who might be in need of her services.

During the meditation portion of the seminar, Connie had felt as if Wayne was gazing directly at her, giving her some kind of message.

By chance, a stroke of fate, or another "connection" meant to be, Connie bypassed the long line of fans and started a new line.

She then became the first to get an autograph from Wayne. If Connie hadn't made that move, she would have missed meeting Janet and me in the lobby. I ended up being the recipient of the card Connie had gone back into her house to retrieve.

I soon began yoga lessons with Connie. After my third session, I was able to take much larger steps, and I feel that I walk almost normally now.

Following that third session, Connie and I engaged in conversation about my progress. All of a sudden she blurted out the words, "You'll see it when you believe it!"

I said, "Connie, do you realize that you just cited the exact title of one of Wayne's best-selling books?" That book just happened to be about personal transformation, the subject we were talking about. She had no idea Wayne had written such a book.

Connie believes, as Wayne does, that we are in control of our bodies and how we react to stress. Diagnosed with systemic lupus at age thirty-two, Connie used yoga as a means to control this disease. Through yoga, she managed to reduce her daily medication intake of thirty-eight pills to one pill. Eventually, Connie rid her body of the disease totally and was able to return to work full-time, entirely free of any medication.

Connie and I developed a very special friendship right from the beginning. I felt so at-ease with her. It was as if I had known her my entire lifetime. That friendship spread throughout both of our families and continues today. Janet has joined us in our weekly yoga sessions.

One more thing about Connie that deserves a little more ink. After reading a couple of my stories, she wanted to see more of my writing. She spurred me to continue writing with her positive comments: "David, you are a writer" and "Writers write." I have since written several short stories, a few of which have been published in local newspapers. I only began writing after incurring Parkinson's at the age of sixty-nine, but that is another story.

I continue to take the medications for Parkinson's disease as prescribed, but I feel that I have conquered the walking part through the power of yoga and believing. I'm also constantly amazed by the positive connections I've made inadvertently through Wayne. As Connie and Wayne both say: "You'll see it when you believe it."

‖ Chapter 15 ‖

Forgiveness Sets You Free

Earlier in the year, Janet received a "friend" invitation on Facebook from Steven Vollick. I told her he must be a relative, as Vollick is my mother's maiden name. Turns out that Steve and I are fifth cousins, and he's conducted extensive research on the Vollick family tree, all the way back to the 1460s.

Steve sent me a photograph taken at a 1939 family reunion. It was a clear picture, despite its age. Janet enlarged the photo and had it printed on nice, glossy paper. As she looked closely at the fifty-eight people in this photograph, she pointed to one and said, "This looks like you."

When I looked at the man she pointed to, I was stunned. I saw the spitting image of myself in Melvin Lyle Dyer, the man I still cannot bring myself to call Dad, Pop, or Father.

Sitting in front of MLD is my brother Jim, who would have been two. At that time, I would have been ten months old, and Wayne, nine months short of being born. I called Wayne with the news of this discovery, and he was amazed at the timing. At that moment, he had been thinking about MLD.

In a previous chapter, I discussed Wayne's struggle with MLD and his eventual forgiveness of the man who had left us and torn our family apart. My feelings toward MLD are ambiguous. I don't know if I'll ever want or be able to forgive him. I'm not sure it will even ever matter.

I do know, however, when I finally faced my painful past and began sharing my story, Wayne told me I wouldn't be completely free until I could forgive myself of any faults or past transgressions I harbored.

"You must learn to love yourself before you can truly begin to love others," he said.

Acceptance would be another key to realizing total freedom.

About two years after being diagnosed with Parkinson's disease, I was involved in a car accident. I, of course, should not have been driving, but I was not ready to give up the freedom driving oneself embodies. I continue to thank God that no one was injured in the accident. I gave up my driver's license the next day, and my wonderful wife Janet became my wheels, among many other things. I wrote a story about the accident and blamed the accident on Parkinson's. In the story, I vowed to fight that miserable "creature."

Wayne must have known I was writing that story, because as I finished the closing, he called. I read him the story over the phone, and he gave me what turned out to be some very valuable advice. He told me I shouldn't waste my time fighting the creature. I should embrace it and put my total belief in any positives I realize from this disease.

Positives realized from an incurable, life-altering disease? Well, yes, there are a few. I believe Parkinson's has brought out my ability to write and tell stories. I have been able to use those precious words that have always been a part of me, words that came to me so easily—even when I had faltered in school—and have returned with such ease after I lifted the cloud of alcohol that had obscured them for years. Those precious words have enabled me to express my love for my brother Wayne through this book. Yes, that is the positive aspect I see and feel in this disease. I don't know if there are any others afflicted with this disease who may feel this way, but it all goes back to that magical word that Wayne and I have both often written: *believe.*

‖ Chapter 16 ‖

Nostalgic Ride Evokes Special Gift

Wayne came to the Detroit area this past summer to give a seminar. While here, he happened to have a rare free day available. He invited me to go with him on a nostalgic trip to our childhood homes. Together we drove to the cottage in Sombra, Ontario, where we had once enjoyed many fond and a few harrowing memories. We proceeded to Mt. Clemens and drove down Town Hall Road past the boarding home where we had once lived with Mr. and Mrs. Scarf.

Then we stopped by the small townhouse-style duplex on Moross where we'd lived after our family was finally reunited. The home was now occupied by a young African-American couple and their teenage daughter. We knocked on the door. William and his daughter Mary answered. Wayne introduced us and explained that we had lived in this house back in the 1950s. They graciously invited us inside and allowed us to look around.

Memories flooded back as we walked through the house. The nine-by-nine upstairs bedroom I had shared with Jim and Wayne now belonged to Mary, a student at Denby High School. Three of us had squeezed into this tiny room that wasn't even big enough for Mary's things.

We checked out the attic where Mother had hid our Christmas presents. We were astonished that the house remained almost the same after all those years. The terrace connecting the kitchen and dining room was just like it had been more than fifty years earlier. The refrigerator was in the same spot, and the kitchen table and ping-pong table in the basement were the same ones we had left behind when we moved out.

We walked through the basement where we used to sit and listen to Tigers baseball games. I pointed out the spot to William where I had been sitting when Virgil Trucks pitched his second no-hitter of the year in 1952. I also commented on the basement steps where we'd sat on Sunday mornings and shined our shoes.

Wayne told William that we had never needed a key to enter the house. He described how we would climb up to the top of the roof and down the other side until we reached the roof of the terrace. From there, we'd climb through the bedroom window.

While there, we spent time chatting with the current residents, learning about their lives and their struggles. We discovered that William had lost his job some time ago and that his unemployment benefits would expire soon. His wife, who was off at work, supplemented the household income with her meager earnings, which were barely above minimum wage.

When Wayne asked Mary about her future aspirations, she seemed to think her reality would be working full-time at McDonalds, perhaps eventually becoming a manager.

As we were leaving, Wayne pointed to what looked like a crumpled dollar lying in the driveway. William picked it up and carefully unfolded what turned out to be a one-hundred-dollar bill. Wayne told him that if he'd found that in his driveway, he'd take his family out somewhere nice to dinner. The tears in William's eyes were real. He thought he was dreaming.

As we approached our car, Wayne stopped and said he'd forgotten something. We walked back to the house where Wayne approached Mary. He told her that since she was living in his house, sleeping in his bedroom, and attending his high school, she couldn't stop there. He then presented her with a scholarship to attend his alma mater, Wayne State University. After seeing Mary's reaction, even my tears were real.

‖ Chapter 17 ‖

Munificent Means Wayne

I started to write a short story that would show what a generous person my brother Wayne has been to me. As I began writing, the word *munificent* seemed to come from my pen.

I have never used that word, nor could I ever remember hearing it used before. I just seemed to know that it was not only the correct word to use in this story but also that it was spelled correctly. I do not have a dictionary in front of me, so I'll just use it.

So how munificent has Wayne been to me? I'll briefly explain, beginning with the one incident that stands above all others in my memory. In 1962, while stationed at Fort Bliss, Texas, I was returning to the barracks from a bar in El Paso. It was late at night, and I heard someone ask me a question. I ignored them and kept walking. I was soon hit in the back of my head with an object of some sort. As I fell to the ground, I broke my wrist. My wallet and watch were stolen. My wallet had only five dollars in it, and that had to last me the rest of the month, which was about two weeks away. My monthly pay then was seventy-eight dollars per month.

The very next day I received a letter from Wayne that he had sent to me from Guam. I hadn't heard from or spoken to Wayne in the past three years at that time. Inside that letter was a five-dollar bill.

He stated in his letter, "I know what it's like being an E1. I'm sure you can use this five-spot." I don't believe I ever thanked Wayne for that five-spot. I had to use it at that time, but eventually I replaced it with a five-spot that I have forever cherished.

Here are a few other examples of his later munificence:

- If I ever needed a vacation, whether it be a trip to Florida or a Caribbean cruise, the money was there.

- If I needed a new car, a new car was there.

- If I needed a condo, a condo was there.

- If I needed a bigger house, a bigger house was there.

- If I needed a new computer, a new computer was there.

- If my son needed money for college, the grand total of all expenditures for four years was there.

By the way, I did look up the word *munificent*. Webster defines it as "extremely generous." I'd rather use my own words and define it as "my brother Wayne."

‖ Chapter 18 ‖

The Unbroken Bonds of Brotherhood

Although Wayne and I live thousands of miles apart (he resides in Hawaii and I in Michigan), we share a deep bond that distance and time cannot diminish. I feel as close to him today as I did many years ago when it was just he and I against the world.

In closing, I'd like to expound upon those nine words frequently uttered by my brother, words that managed to change my life for the better.

"Do not die with your music still in you!"

I don't know who first coined that phrase, but I do know who delivered that message to me. At age sixty-nine, those words resulted in a dramatic change in my life and a happiness and freedom I hadn't known for a long time. I guess I'm proof that you're never too old to change.

Wayne, while you've always been the one to offer words of wisdom, I'd like to share a bit of advice. Don't stop delivering that special message that impacted me so much.

It would be difficult to put a number on how many people you've inspired throughout the years. I know I'm definitely on that list of the thousands you've reached and

103

touched. I'll always treasure all the memories we've shared since the early days, from sliding around on the ice on Piper Street until now. I love you, and I'm so proud to be your big brother.

●

****

Part 2 My Time to Touch:
Short Stories and Poems by David L. Dyer

~

My friend Pamela Frucci, who also happens to be the co-chair of the creative writing club I belong to, gave me an article written by Michael J. Fox. It turns out Michael J. Fox and I share several things in common. I was a high school dropout. So was Michael J. Fox. I quit high school in the 12th grade. So did Michael J. Fox. I have Parkinson's disease. So does Michael J. Fox. Do the similarities ever end? Not yet. I find myself his mirror image as I quote Michael J. Fox:

"Parkinson's is a perfect metaphor for the lack of control. Every unwanted movement in my hand or arm, every twitch that I cannot anticipate or arrest reminds me that even in the domain of my own being I am not calling the shots with no escape from the disease, its symptoms and its challenges. I was forced to resort to acceptance. My happiness grows in direct proportion to my acceptance and in inverse proportion to my expectation."

Very powerful words, don't you think? I would love to be able to read to Michael J. Fox the story you are about to read, which entails my first four years with Parkinson's.

Living with Parkinson's

In August of 2007, I was diagnosed with Parkinson's disease. I researched this disease and discovered that not only was it incurable, but my condition would worsen as time went on. My immediate reaction was complete denial, and I continued drinking. The prescribed medication didn't seem to be working. In fact, it seemed to have a negative effect when combined with alcohol.

It took almost a year, some personal counseling and nine magical words from my brother Wayne, "Do not die with your music still in you," for me to tell my Vietnam story. I finally revealed those harrowing experiences that I had concealed within me for the past 37 years. After doing so, it felt like a ton of bricks had been lifted from me. At this point, I'd been diagnosed with Parkinson's for around a year now. While my physical condition had shown no improvement, mentally I felt so much better after releasing my Vietnam story and putting it on paper.

Let's go back for a moment to those words describing Parkinson's disease: incurable and worsen. Since I was writing a story and didn't want to stifle my creative flow, I asked Janet to look up the definition of the word *worse*. She informed me it meant *bad, harmful or unpleasant.*

Throughout our lives, Wayne has often told me that I've always possessed the ability to write. However, whatever gifts or talents I possessed, would always take a secondary role to alcohol which seemed to always have complete control of me.

Parkinson's disease forced me to quit drinking. And after going on the wagon, I suffered terrible bouts of insomnia as the lack of alcohol kept me awake at night. It was during those sleepless nights, that I began writing and unleashed a prolific stream of stories and poems. *What could be bad, harmful or unpleasant about that?*

Now let's go to October of 2008. At one of Wayne's seminars, I met Connie Fedel, a wonderful woman whose personal story could dwarf mine. Her story has yet to be written. I use the word "yet" in hopes that someday I will be able to do so.

Connie is a yoga instructor. Today, almost four years after meeting her, Janet and I continue taking our weekly yoga sessions from Connie. At the beginning, Connie marveled at the way my Vietnam story was written and wanted to see more of my writing. She told me, "David, you are a writer," and added "writer's write." I then began writing one story after another. She seems to be touched by just about everything I write, and her inspiration deeply touches me. *Is that so bad, harmful or unpleasant?*

To date, I have written close to fifty short stories. Most are inspirational and about family members or friends. And now, I've written this book.

During these past four years, since incurring Parkinson's, I have made four trips to Florida to visit my mother. How lucky I am to be able to visit my mother at the age of 72 and take her to dinner and watch a baseball game with her as we celebrated her 95th birthday?

During this time, I've also come to realize and truly believe that there is a God. There is no way I would have stopped drinking on my own. I tried too many times to no avail. As Parkinson's was entering my body, the alcohol was slowly exiting. I thank God for allowing me to survive another 40 years since Vietnam and to begin writing at the age of 69. This brings me to what I call my signature four line poem:

> When I vowed to give up alcohol
> Which was my life long crutch
> I was given a brand new life
> It became my time to touch

Bad? Harmful? Unpleasant? Now that I've lived with this incurable disease for the better part of four years, I believe I have completely dispelled the notion that Parkinson's disease is the "worst" thing to happen to me. If you don't believe this you certainly will when you read what I'm about to write as I close this story.

As I stated earlier in this book, I retired from the Army in 1982 after 21 years of service. I'm not going to reveal any dollar amounts, but my retirement pension was 52 per cent of my active duty pay. That, of course, was not enough to live on even though I was single at the time.

For the next 29 years, I continued to receive regular cost-of-living increases, which now coupled with social security provide me a livable retirement income. Recently though, the Veteran's Administration determined that my Parkinson's disease is connected to Agent Orange, a toxic chemical used to flush out the enemy in Vietnam. Because of this connection, the VA has awarded me Combat Related Specialty Pay that has doubled my retirement income overnight. *Bad? Harmful? Unpleasant?*

So this has been my life these past four years since receiving the fateful diagnosis known as Parkinson's disease. Since I've done away with the word "worse," I look forward at the age of 72 to seeing what the next four years may bring. Meanwhile, I'll ask Janet to look up another word for me, "incurable."

A Revelation
Or Something Happened This Past Christmas Eve

In order to tell this story the way I want to I must refer to the closing of my previous story, *Living with Parkinson's*. I closed that story with these words: Since I've done away with the word "worse" I look forward, at the age of 72, to seeing what the next four years may bring.

My first four years with Parkinson's completely dispelled the word "worse" since everything that was happening was just the opposite. I was writing short stories that were actually touching others. I was alcohol free and saving the best for last - I found God. It had to have been God who helped me quit drinking. I never would have stopped on my own. I was 68 years old. Yes, God knows all, and he wasn't about to let me die with my music still in me.

Again, I asked Janet to look up the word "incurable" for me. She said it meant "a disease with no possibility of cure." No possibility? Remember now I have found God. God is the opposite of worse. God is good. With God all things are possible.

I began my second four years living with Parkinson's by taking a routine stress test that turned up abnormal results. A heart catherization indicated I had severe heart blockages and needed to undergo bypass surgery as soon as possible. Once again, God was with me throughout a successful surgery and the several months of recovery. Once I was well enough, I joined the Grosse Ile Presbyterian Church. Not only did I join the church, I joined a new family of about 300 members and developed many new friendships.

Incidentally, after recovering from surgery, I am now able to rise from a sitting position to a standing position without assistance. This was something I could not do prior to heart surgery. Previously, I was told by my neurologist that this was a trait of Parkinson's disease. He was as amazed as me to see this result. Yesterday, I walked two and a half miles without resting. I've also managed to write this book.

All of what I've written about here is what my life has been during the first six months of my second four years with Parkinson's. If all that is incurable then I don't want to be cured. I might add that all of this is only a lead in to what has happened since this past Christmas Eve.

This story begins as I recall my favorite Christmas song of all time, *O Holy Night*. I must have heard that song somewhere, or sometime, in my very early years. Every year, during the holiday season, I yearn to hear this song.

I have often said and written that my earliest memory was at age four. I remember sliding on the ice, playing marbles, and the Murphy bed that came out of the wall, engulfing the entire room. My memory stops at that point and doesn't return until age seven when Wayne and I were boarded at a home in Mt Clemens. Previously, we had been boarded in a couple of other homes, but those memories have been somehow permanently suppressed. That seems strange, because the suppression of all the death and destruction I witnessed in Vietnam came back some 37 years later when I began talking and writing about them.

I have often said that I began school in the third grade, and that has always been my steadfast belief as I do not remember any schooling prior to then.

Something happened this past Christmas Eve, though, that unlocked a sliver of those unknown years. Janet, David-Scott and I attended midnight church service as we have done for the past several years. This time I was especially tired as David-Scott and I spent most of the day going back and forth to the local mall, but that is another story.

I asked Janet to watch over me closely during the service since the medication I was taking caused me to doze off. Sure enough, a lapse in the service was enough for me to close my eyes and relax. Janet missed the queue. Although, I wasn't sleeping, I was in a daze as I listened to the music. Suddenly, the beautiful voice of a female vocalist captured my attention, and I became mesmerized as I heard her sing the words to *O Holy Night*. Janet then elbowed me, and I fully awakened as the words "Fall on your knees" were belted out. To me, this was an electrifying performance.

When the service was over, I asked Janet if she knew the name of the vocalist. She told me her name was Michelle Lepidi. When we returned home, I looked up Michelle's email in our church directory and sent her a brief note thanking her for the beautiful rendition of my favorite Christmas song. I told her that the timing was just perfect and once again thanked her for the wonderful Christmas present. I also mentioned that it was 66 years ago when I first heard that song. I don't know where that figure came from, but read on.

A couple of days later, I received a response from Michelle. She thanked me for what I had written about her and was happy to hear that I enjoyed her solo. I then sent her a copy of a story I had written about her friend, Pamela Frucci, who is also in the choir, Jim Parker, the music director and myself which described the connection between the three of us. Michelle replied and agreed with the point of my story, that there are no accidents when it comes to meeting certain people.

She then explained a series of fateful circumstances that led up to her Christmas Eve performance. She praised God for leading her to Jim Parker, her vocal coach. Without his instruction, she would never be able to sing the songs she sings. On Christmas Eve, she was scheduled to sing solos at both services, but began having trouble with her voice. She didn't think her first performance measured up to her

standards. Distraught over the situation, she went home
between services to try and rest her voice. Unfortunately,
due to severe vocal nodules and a flare up of asthma, Michelle
couldn't clear her throat and regain her voice. It was then that
she looked in the mirror and prayed to God that her next
performance would be to his glory.

God was there. I do not see how anyone could have put
on a better performance that night than she did. I may not be
a musical expert, but I was so moved by the performance of
someone I didn't even know – moved enough to want to let
her know the effect it had on me at that particular moment.
This is where I believe our connection came to fore. The
timing was just perfect.

Following that performance, Michelle couldn't sing
again, and the day after Christmas she was in the hospital
undergoing surgery. While in the hospital, she read my first
email and later told me it meant the world to her. She even
showed it to her husband and said, "This is why I sing."

A few days later, I wrote a short story in honor of my
mother's 96th birthday which I'll deliver in April. I ended the
story with these words: "Mother, it is a wonderful feeling for
me to know when I've created a welling or tears of happiness
in your eyes as you read stories that I have written. I'll bet
Michelle would join me in saying that is why I write. "

I sent Michelle a copy of the story, and her response was
moving and emotional. She said the story made her cry, in a
healing way. She felt honored that I took the time to let her
know what an impact she has had on me. She thanked me for
motivating her to get it together and begin singing again.

Three nights ago, I gathered up all of the emails and
retired to David-Scott's room where I read them once again
as I lay on his bed. I then put all of my thoughts on this past
Christmas Eve and soon fell asleep. Sometime, during the
next hour, I had a vision. I saw myself as a little boy sitting
on a hardwood floor with my legs folded. I stared straight
ahead at a woman singing *O Holy Night*. I couldn't take my

eyes off of her. Later I gazed around the room and noticed other children sitting there watching her just as I was in what appeared to be a classroom setting. As soon as I stood up in my dream, I woke up.

Though, I have no other memories from that early age, I now know where and when I first heard that song. Yes, it would have been 66 years ago. That song has stayed with me my entire lifetime and I now know that I must have attended school prior to the third grade.

Thank you, Michelle, for your part in whatever it was that happened this past Christmas Eve.

Janet, me and David-Scott

My Mother, Hazel and David-Scott

My brother Jim, his wife, Marilyn, Janet and me

Janet and me

David L. Dyer

Janet and me

David L. Dyer

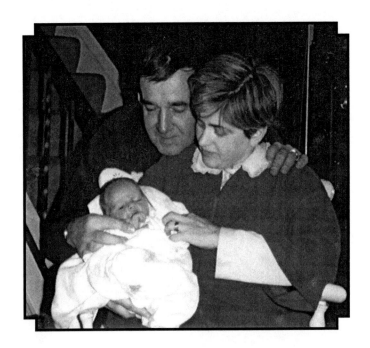

Our first Christmas together

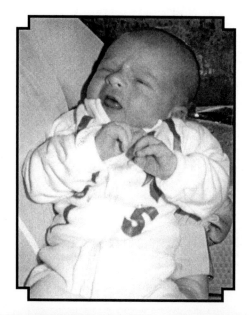

David-Scott born 1986

Connie Fedel, My Yoga instructor and good friend

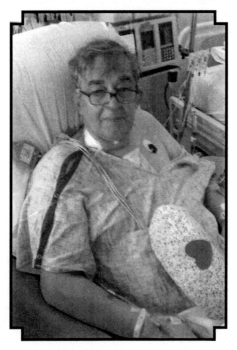

Following by-pass surgery

Play On Words

At our last creative writers club meeting our co-chairwoman, Pamela Frucci, brought in a painting of a statue of a man whose arms were wrapped around his shoulders. He appeared to be deep in thought. She told us that the new Grosse Ile High School principal displayed that painting as inspiration for his students. Another writer's club member, Michelle Horvath, took a picture of the painting and emailed it to all of us. Our assignment was to write about what we saw or felt as we viewed the photo.

I sat down at the midnight hour, placed the photo on the table in front of me and stared at it. I didn't take my eyes off of it for about 30 minutes at which time I picked up my pen and began writing. The first words that came from my pen and my thoughts were a play on words. Yes, that was a story I just had to re-write. I took a couple of my older stories and somewhat combined them. Bear with me! I think you are going to enjoy reading this.

Did you know there are over 100,000 words in the English dictionary? Probably as many as 75 per cent of the same words have been used in all of the stories I have written. I might add that I doubt if I even use more than a couple of hundred of those 100,000 words that are available. I could probably say the same for others that write, including famous authors. Writers do not invent words as they write. The same words are simply moved around to create a totally different meaning. They are at times changed for the same purpose. That is the miracle of words. The shifting of words abruptly changes story lines.

There are several words in the dictionary that are spelled exactly the same but have totally different meanings. There is even a descriptive word for those words. They are called homographs. Here are a few of them: There – Change – Play – Foot – Run – Right – Step – Store – Class – Bill. No wonder it is so difficult for foreigners to learn the English language.

Now let's make a comparison. We'll take any one of those 100,000 words and compare it to a simple leaf upon a tree. The branches on a tree create thousands of leaves. When the cold weather arrives the leaves begin falling. The wind may whisk them straight ahead, to the left or to the right. Many of them will touch and make a connection. Some will touch leaves of another tree and make a connection. The leaf that touches no other will die alone. Think about that, it rarely happens.

So where is the equation? First, we must define a word. What is a word? A word is a word and nothing else, at least until it is paired with another word. If a word is written and is not paired with another it will be useless, have little meaning and eventually will be trashed, and just as that leaf that fell from that tree, it will die alone.

When a single word is paired with another and another it begins to gain strength. Soon the words become sentences. The strength and power they could yield would depend on what words were used and how they were put together. They could simply be two, three, four or five letter words randomly chosen. Here is an example: I will use nine words in this example and since I am writing this story, I will pick the words. They are: With – You – In – Die - Your – Do – Still – Not – Music. I shuffled those words around many times. I was determined to create a sensible sentence using those words. It finally worked as they eventually came together in this fashion: Do not die with your music still in you.

Now I am going to tell you something very serious as I take a break from playing with words in this paragraph only and then we'll return. I do not know from where those words were originally put together that way, but I do know that it was my brother Wayne that uttered them to me. They were not only powerful words, they were life altering.

Eight of those words are known as homonyms while one of them remains nameless. Those eight words are spelled differently and have totally different meanings than their counterparts, yet they are pronounced exactly the same. Here they are: Dew – knot – dye – withe[1] - yore' - mucic[2]- still – inn – ewe.

Notice that the word *still* is the only one that is not a homonym. Could that mean that I may *still* have a few songs yet to sing?

I wonder how many homographs there are in 100,000 words. I listed ten of them in the first part of this story. There is one that I left off of that list, yet I used it several times. That is the word *touch*. It is a homograph. It does have two separate meanings, yet they are spelled the same.

I wrote about leaves falling from a tree and touching others. I mentioned the consequences of the leaf that failed to touch another and also of a word that was never paired.

Let me define the word *touch*. First, it is to put your finger or hand on an object or a person. The other definition, in my words, is to be emotionally moved with a creation of a welling in your eyes. This could be from reading a book, watching a movie, etc. In touching others, it could be to create that welling in their eyes as they are being emotionally moved by reading something that you have written.

---

1   flexible twig of willow used for binding pronounced with

2   colorless crystalline acid pronounced musik

David L. Dyer

It took 68 years of my life, the incurable disease called Parkinson's, some personal counseling, nine magical words from my brother Wayne, and the trading of my very best friend on my knees at the wall of the Vietnam Memorial for sobriety, before I could and did begin writing short stories that began touching others.

Yes, several of my stories have touched others. How do I know that? A number of people have told me of the welling they have incurred from reading my stories. I'm going to close this story with three stanzas of poetry I wrote exactly one year ago today.

> When I vowed to give up alcohol
> Which was my life long crutch
> I was given a brand new life
> It became my time to touch
>
> Now as I compare my life to that
> Of a leaf upon a tree
> Take a good look at that tree
> And tell me what you see
>
>
> The weather's cold
> The leaves have fallen
> And some of them have blown
> But I can take solace in knowing
> I'll never die alone

A Valentine to my Wife

I've done a lot of writing
These past couple of years
When reading some of the stories again
I sometimes fight back tears

There's a story I wrote a year ago
That seems to have been buried
Without a doubt it's my favorite one
It was to the girl I married

The closing of that story is
Very much worth repeating
I'm sure that you'll agree with me
It's better than any card's greeting

I wrote a story titled *The Most Beautiful Girl in the World*. That story began with Webster's definition of the words beauty and beautiful. I summed up those definitions with three words of my own: *My Wife Janet*.

Here it is as I wrote the closing of *The Most Beautiful Girl in the World*. Since I'm not being graded on my grammar, I am going to close with one single sentence. It will be a rather lengthy one. It may have a few commas or capital letters, but there will not be a single period. The reason I am doing this is to honor the fact that every word in this closing statement means so much to me that inserting a period anywhere would not do it justice. Here it goes:

Janet, you have not only become the love of my life you have given completely of yourself to become such as terrific mother, you began to read to David-Scott six months before he was even born, this practice became a ritual that would continue nightly for several years, I'm sure that this was the beginning of whatever it was that instilled such a love of reading into David-Scott, a love that would in turn allow him to be so successful in his academic life, I credit you entirely for all of what he learned right up until the time that he became more intelligent than either of us, I am so proud to say that David-Scott has recently graduated magna cum laude from the very prestigious Alma College, now as this never ending sentence continues, the following words go much deeper than what appears on the surface, as our Silver Anniversary approaches and as I look into your eyes today, I continue to see and feel as Webster so eloquently defined, but again in my own words, *The Most Beautiful Girl in the World*

Whenever I read back those words,
Chills run up my spine
I've never felt so honored and proud,
To be your Valentine.

Love David

This is a birthday card I wrote to my yoga instructor and very dear friend Connie Fedel. It will not need any further explanation.

Happy Birthday Connie

As I sit here pondering what to write
It really shouldn't be hard
To express in words my gratitude
To you on your birthday card

My thoughts take me back a few years
To shortly after we met
You told me of your systemic lupus
And that story amazes me yet

How you took complete control of your life
And then you began to live
A life that wouldn't have any limits
And how you began to give

From soup kitchens to Fish and Loaves
To yoga and what's more
Whenever you sensed there was a need
You never closed the door

The twelfth of October of two thousand eight
Was the day that we met
We began weekly yoga sessions
And those sessions continue yet

We became the best of friends
From that very first day
That friendship spread throughout our families
And even continues today

131

So I'll close by saying how grateful I am
And I thank you so very much
You've become much more than my yoga instructor
You've taught me how to touch

Your friend David Dyer

While Janet and David-Scott were vacationing in Florida, I was home alone for a week. Janet's birthday was coming soon. Since I told her I don't buy greeting cards anymore, because I don't feel right signing my name to someone else's words, I'm sure she was expecting some kind of special creation. I was lying on the couch watching a ballgame on TV and soon fell asleep. When I awoke, the game was over, and I stared at the mantle clock. I was giving deep thought to what I'd write to Janet for her birthday. While staring at the clock, I remembered buying that clock in Frankenmuth, Michigan in 1988. I thought more about the year 1988 which was the year we moved into this house. Then, I thought no, the year of 1986 was the most exciting year of both our lives. I reached for my pen at 1 a.m. and began writing.

Nineteen Eighty-Six

As I stare at the mantel and look at the clock
And listen as the hand ticks
My thoughts take me back to that wonderful year
Of nineteen eighty-six

When the clock struck twelve on the very first night
Of that memorable year
We were at a New Year's party
And we seemed to disappear

That was our first trip to Florida
And we stayed at the home of my mother
The New Year's party that we attended
Was at the home of my brother

That spring you helped make a dreary job fun
As I will never forget
The Saturday mornings you helped me deliver
The Troy Somerset Gazette

I was living in the condo then
And you were still up north
We soon put an end to all that travel
As we married on April fourth

It seemed we'd accomplished a lot at that point
But we found it was just the beginning
If we compared the year to a baseball game
We'd be only in the first inning

It wasn't long before we'd notice
The change in your condition
Into our house we'd welcome soon
A very much wanted addition

I remember the day you told me that
We were going to have a boy
I remember holding you very close
As my heart was filled with joy

At that time in our lives, there were many things
That were not very clear
But I'll try to chronologically tell
The story of that wonderful year

We called him "little David"
And I vividly remember the sight
And the sounds as I listened and watched you reading
A story to him every night

Though he wouldn't be born for another six months
He certainly got a head start
That undying love you had for him
Continued to tug at my heart

A few days later, my brother Jim came over
With Marilyn, his lovely wife
That visit turned historical for me
As it completely changed my life

Marilyn hooked me up with a guy named Tony
Who worked for a company called Smart
I began copying medical records
With a copier I'd wheel on a cart

Now "little David" continued to grow
And in November of eighty-six
I remember so well you lying down
Doing nothing but counting his kicks

It was then decided you would go with me
As I copied records each day
Since we'd always be at a hospital
We felt much safer that way

One week later as we were copying records
Tony Arnold paid us a visit
He introduced us to a lady named Karen
Whose looks were so very exquisite

Tony was leaving but it didn't seem
To be much of a loss
Especially when he told me that
Karen would now be my boss

An everlasting friendship began
As we met with her that day
A friendship that continues
And I still work for her today

It's been twenty-four years since that day we met
And she stands above all others
She's like the sister I never had
And I love her as I do my brothers

David L. Dyer

Now it was time to give "little David" a name
So we threw names into a pot
The names that seemed to surface the most
Were of David and also of Scott

As we were copying on the tenth of December
You said it was time to go
I asked if I could finish this chart
You emphatically told me no

Off to Henry Ford we went
And later that same day
Labor was induced and David-Scott
Would soon be on his way

It was shortly after six p.m.
As I stood next to the nurse
It was then I witnessed a miracle
He decided to come out head first

I walked with the nurse over to the sink
Where she cleaned him very fast
Then she put him in my hands
That sensation would forever last

I told you that he was beautiful
But you couldn't see him yet
As soon as you were able to
It was a sight you would never forget

We went to our home in Sterling Heights
And regardless of the cold weather
We could not have been happier
As we spent our first Christmas together

So that was the year of eighty-six
And all I could remember
Of how things happened from the first of January
'Til the last day of December

Again as I gaze at the mantel clock
A timer rings to give me a warning
It's time to take my morning pills
It's now five o'clock in the morning

Happy Birthday,

Love David

Following emergency bypass surgery, I was released from the hospital after four days. Janet then became my nurse, in addition to everything else. To show my appreciation, I wrote her the following poem.

To the Love of my Life

Not Parkinson's nor a few heart felt incisions
Could ever drive us apart
No knife could ever pierce the space
I've reserved for you in my heart

Thank you God for pulling me through
I know that you've blessed me again
My fourth life began some four years ago
As I let the words flow from my pen

I've been lifted from hell and I'm halfway to heaven
Let's take a brief pause from that ride
I don't believe I'd have made it this far
Without having you by my side

It's been over a quarter century now
Since the day that we tied the knot
Soon after came the love of our lives
The birth of David-Scott

There've been ups and downs,
There've been highs and lows
But no storm that we couldn't weather
No matter what the obstacle was
We managed through it together

David L. Dyer

Now as the days continue to pass
We can look at each other with pride
And no matter what the future may bring
That knot will always be tied

Last year it seemed like the spring season just passed us by. We had wintry weather right into the month of May. There were, however, a few sightings of spring between the winter and summer months, and this poem is about one of those rare sightings.

Spring

Many have said spring passed by us this year
Because the wintry weather
My wife and I will dispel those words
As we share what we've witnessed together

March 21st and the sight of a robin
Always seems to make that connection
And despite the falling temperatures
This year would be no exception

On March 21st Janet spotted a robin
That seemed to be building a nest
There was nothing, not even the very cold weather
To prevent her from seeking her quest

She flew past our window to the front of our house
Where she nestled in one of the trees
From there she carried the equipment she needed
To build her nest with such ease

She built her nest on our window sill
Up high in one little section
Located on top of one of the meters
Of our electrical connection

Soon we spotted three little eggs
In the middle of her nest
We watched as she was sitting on them
She seemed to need lots of rest

Now yesterday was Mother's Day
And also the middle of spring
As we gaze into that nest today
What a wonderful feeling it brings

Those three little eggs are now three little birds
And they wait with their mouths wide apart
I watch as the robin feeds them one at a time
And I feel a slight tug at my heart

So don't ever say that spring passed us by
You really don't have to look hard
Just wait for the date and look for the robin
Then look in your own backyard

I will close this book with words that bring back all the memories of Vietnam, or maybe the memories never left. This is how I spent Christmas Eve in 1970.

The Night before Christmas in South Vietnam, 1970

'Twas the night before Christmas
Forty-one year ago
The monsoon erased
Any thoughts of snow

I wondered what kind
Of a night it would be
With continuous sounds
Of artillery

Christmas was coming
As I looked at the clock
But there was nary a chimney
To hang up a sock

Past Christmas memories
Quickly passed through my head
As I climbed from the bunker
And lay down on my bed

Soon the sirens went off
And arose such a clatter
We rushed to the ER
To see what was the matter

David L. Dyer

Four incoming wounded
Were already here
And two KIAs[3]
Brought up the rear

I looked out the door
And gazed up at a star
As the four wounded soldiers
Went to the OR[4]

They were all involved
In some type of explosion
This was not the life
That they had chosen

They all were drafted
And had no choice
But their MDWs[5]
Gave cause to rejoice

The death and destruction
That still lay ahead
Told me I still
Had plenty to dread

There were no obstacles
Or coursers to fly
It must have been God
Way up in that sky

It was now past midnight
And Christmas was here
I celebrated
By drinking a beer

---

3   Killed in Action

4   Operating Room

5   Million Dollar Wound. An injury severe enough for the soldier
to be sent home.

Once again I lay
Down on my bed
While visions of mortar rounds
Danced in my head

I'd think happy thoughts
And closed my eyes with a grin
But in just a few hours
A new day would begin